THE BRITANNICA GUIDE TO THE SOCIAL SCIENCES

POLITICAL SCIENCE

EDITED BY

ANN HOSEIN

Britannica
Educational Publishing

IN ASSOCIATION WITH

ROSEN
EDUCATIONAL SERVICES

Published in 2016 by Britannica Educational Publishing (a trademark of Encyclopædia Britannica, Inc.) in association with The Rosen Publishing Group, Inc.
29 East 21st Street, New York, NY 10010

To see additional Britannica Educational Publishing titles, go to rosenpublishing.com.

First Edition

Britannica Educational Publishing
J.E. Luebering: Director, Core Reference Group
Anthony L. Green: Editor, Compton's by Britannica

Rosen Publishing
Ann Hosein: Editor
Nelson Sá: Art Director
Brian Garvey: Designer
Cindy Reiman: Photography Manager
Rona Tuccillo: Photo Researcher

Cataloging-in-Publication Data

Political science / edited by Ann Hosein.
    pages cm — (The Britannica guide to the social sciences)
Includes bibliographical references and index.
ISBN 978-1-62275-546-2 (library bound)
1. Political science—Juvenile literature. I. Hosein, Ann.
JA70.P65 2016
320—dc23

                    2015017695

Manufactured in the United States of America

CONTENTS

Introduction viii
    Fields and Subfields...............................xv

Chapter One
Development of Political Science
from Ancient Times to the Early
20th Century... 1
    Ancient Influences.................................. 1
    Early Modern Developments................. 3
    19th-Century Roots of Contemporary
    Political Science....................................... 6
    The Early 20th Century: Developments
    in the United States................................ 8
    The Early 20th Century: Developments
    Outside the United States......................11
       Other Political Science Scholars 13

2

Chapter Two
Post-World War II Trends in
Political Science.......................................16
    Behavioralism.......................................18
       The Eurobarometer 22
    Political Culture................................... 23
    Systems Analysis 25
    Theory of Rational Choice 27
    Democratic Theory 28

17

Chapter Three
International Relations 31
    Historical Development 31
       Between the Two World Wars 33
       NATO 36

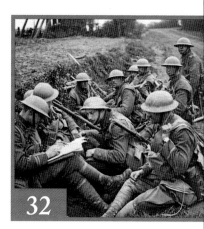

32

The Postwar Ascendancy
of Realism 37
The Behavioral Approach and the
Task of Integration 38
The Later 20th Century 39
Foreign Policy and International
Systems.. 40
The General-System Perspective........41
Constructivism............................... 42
Structures, Institutions, and
Levels of Analysis 42
Constructivism............................... 42
International Political Economy....... 43

Chapter Four
Domestic Politics: Public Opinion 46
Theoretical and Practical
Conceptions 46
The Formation and Change of Public
Opinion 49
Components of Public Opinion:
Attitudes and Values.........................49
Factors Influencing Public Opinion.......51
Environmental Factors......................51
Mass Media 51
Interest Groups................................53
Opinion Leaders..............................53
Complex Influences 54
Al Gore and Public Opinion...............55
Public Opinion and Government 56
Political Polls....................................58
Public Opinion Polling................... 60

Chapter Five
Domestic Politics: Elections 62
Types of Elections 62

Systems of Vote Counting 64
   Legislative Elections........................ 64
   Executive Elections..........................65
Constituencies: Districting and
Apportionment 65
Voting Practices 68
   Secret Voting.................................69
   Balloting..70
   Compulsory Voting 70
   Electoral Abuses 71
Participation in Elections 71
   Voter ID Laws.................................72
Influences on Voting Behaviour 74

Chapter Six
Domestic Politics: Government.............75
Agricultural Society 75
   The Spread of Civilization 76
The City-State of Greece 78
Rome and the Republic.......................78
The Middle Ages 79
   Dissolution and Instability.............. 80
   Feudalism... 80
   The Rise of Law and the
   Nation-State 81
The Rise and Fall of Absolute
Monarchy..83
Representation and
Constitutional Monarchy..................... 84
The American and French
Revolutions 85
Nationalism and Imperialism............... 86
Communism and Fascism.................... 87
Liberal Democracy.............................. 88
Prospects in the 21st Century...............89

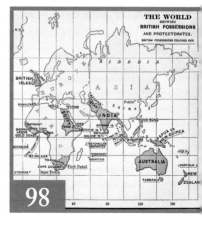

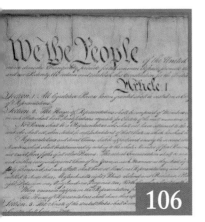

Chapter Seven
Public Administration 91
  Early Systems of Administration 91
    The Song/Sung Dynasty 92
  Modern Developments..........................95
    Prussia 95
    France.. 96
    The British Empire 97
    The United States 99
    The Soviet Union............................100
    China 101
    Japan 101
    Developing Nations 102

Chapter Eight
Constitutional Government.................105
  Features of Constitutional
  Government 105
    Procedural Stability 106
    Accountability 106
    Representation 107
    Division of Power 108
    Openness and Disclosure................108
    Constitutionality 109
    Constitutional Change 110
    Constitutional Stability 112
  The Practice of Constitutional
  Government 113
    Great Britain 113
    United States 116
    Europe.. 116
    British Decolonization and
    Emerging National Constitutions...... 118
    Latin America, Africa, and Asia......120

Chapter Nine
Influential Figures in Political Science 122

Confucius 122

Plato 124

Aristotle 125

Kautilya 126

Ibn Khaldun 127

Niccolò Machiavelli 129

Thomas Hobbes 130

John Locke 132

Jean-Jacques Rousseau 133

Montesquieu 135

Adam Smith 136

Edmund Burke 137

Henri de Saint-Simon 138

Auguste Comte 139

Karl Marx 140

Friedrich Engels 143

Arthur F. Bentley 144

Harold Dwight Lasswell 145

V.O. Key, Jr. 147

William Riker 148

Robert A. Dahl 149

Conclusion 152

Glossary 153

Bibliography 155

Index 168

In 2015, Indiana Governor Mike Pence caught the attention of the country with a "religious freedom" law that stirred up a firestorm in the press and social media. Newspapers, news stations, and media pundits from around the world weighed in on the subject and the new law's legality and implications. What had been a promising political career quickly became radioactive with a future that was murky at best.

Political scientists are racing to determine and quantify the circumstances that have led to a national furor over the law. How did a state's law become the focal point for a larger issue? What

Indiana governor Mike Pence speaks about the Religious Freedom Restoration Act in March 2015.

role did the media play in Governor Pence's freefall? Finding the answers to these questions can define the success or failure of a politician's career, determine popular public opinion, and ultimately shape the laws that govern a nation.

Political science is the systematic study of governance by the application of empirical and generally scientific methods of analysis. As traditionally defined and studied, political science examines the state and its organs and institutions. The contemporary discipline, however, is considerably broader than this, encompassing studies of all the societal, cultural, and psychological factors that mutually influence the operation of government and the body politic.

Although political science borrows heavily from the other social sciences, it is distinguished from them by its focus on power—defined as the ability of one political actor to get another actor to do what he or she wants—at the international, national, and local levels. Political science is generally used in the singular, but in French and Spanish the plural *(sciences politiques* and *ciencias políticas,* respectively) is used, perhaps a reflection of the discipline's eclectic nature. Although political science overlaps considerably with political philosophy, the two fields are distinct. Political philosophy is concerned primarily with political ideas and values, such as rights, justice, freedom, and political obligation (whether people should or should not obey political authority); it is normative in its approach (i.e., it is concerned with what ought to be rather than with what is) and rationalistic in its method. In contrast, political science studies institutions and behaviour, favours the descriptive over the normative, and develops theories or draws conclusions based on empirical observations, which are expressed in quantitative terms where possible.

So how does this play into what happened in Indiana? The controversial legislation, officially called the Religious Freedom Restoration Act (SEA 101), was meant to "ensure religious liberty is fully protected under [Indiana] law," according to Pence. The heart of the law was found in the following clause: "A [state] governmental entity may not substantially burden a person's [defined as an individual, business, religious institution or association] exercise of religion, even if the burden results from a rule of general applicability."

The criticism of the law, and main thrust of critics' arguments, is that the law allows business owners to deny service to groups typically targeted with discrimination. Previous lawsuits in other parts of the country have seen the state side with the customer. Indiana's reaction was to legally support businesses' religious objections. Taken to the logical extreme, say critics, businesses can deny service to people of any religion, sexual orientation, or any other group they choose. Although discrimination could theoretically apply to any group, the debate focused on the gay and lesbian community who traditionally had been targeted by groups based on their moral or religious convictions.

A number of groups mobilized to protest the legislation. This includes other state governors such as Democratic Connecticut governor Dan Malloy who announced an executive order that barred state-funded travel to Indiana. "We are sending a message," said Malloy over social media, "that discrimination won't be tolerated." Seattle's openly gay mayor Ed Murray followed suit with a similar executive order. Local businesses and organizations also expressed concern over the law. The NCAA is headquartered in Indianapolis, and the association's president Mark Emmert said, "we intend to closely examine the implications of this bill and how it might affect future events as well as our workforce."

Businesses that exert a large influence beyond their respective industries joined in the debate as well. Apple CEO Tim Cook wrote in a *Washington Post* op-ed that "America's business community recognized a long time ago that discrimination, in all its forms, is bad for business." Business-rating site Angie's List put a halt to its plan to expand into Indiana, and software company Salesforce canceled all Indiana-based events and travel responsibilities.

The full text of the law went on to define "substantially burden," but it still left real-world implementation of the law up to a court's interpretation. While not explicitly addressing questions about whether the law would permit discrimination, Governor Pence has denied accusations that the law allows the practice.

While Pence may have foreseen that businesses and politicians would react negatively to his predictably controversial law, the media frenzy that followed was probably a surprise to him, his supporters, and political scientists. Almost immediately after the legislation was signed into law, it was condemned on the social media platform Twitter. Media icon, Star Trek actor, and gay rights activist George Takei tweeted on March 27, 2015, "Join me to #BoycottIndiana. Show Gov. #Pence we won't stand for bigotry in the name of religion." A fury of similar sentiments burst forth on Twitter, Facebook, and other social media platforms, all labelling Indiana and its governor as bigoted. Indiana author John Green tweeted, "As a Hoosier, I'm deeply saddened and embarrassed. A government exists to protect its citizens; instead, it is legalizing their oppression." Ironically, even religious groups, such as the Christian Church (Disciples of Christ) which had a convention scheduled to take place in Indianapolis in 2017, decried the law. Former NBA star and current sports analyst Charles Barkley added that, "Discrimination in any form is unacceptable to me. As long as anti-gay legislation exists in any state, I strongly believe big events such as the Final Four and Super Bowl should not be held in those states' cities."

The overwhelming response on social media perfectly illustrates the pluralist and interest-group approach to political science that Arthur F. Bentley, a political scientist in the 1930s and 1950s, was a part of. Bentley credited "group participation" with brining about social movement. What made this one go "viral," was that it was fueled by fast Internet connections and a connected populous.

However, Indiana is not the first state with this type of law, yet none of those states experienced the type of media attention paid to Governor Pence's legislation. He made that very point in a televised interview, but it was too late for Pence. The state's religious freedom law launched a national debate over the law's perceived acquiescence to discrimination against gays and lesbians.

Over time politicians and officials have become aware of the media's role in shaping and swaying a public debate over many policy issues. But why these issues are thrust into the media spotlight in the first place is still a subject debated by political scientists. President Obama's health-care law was a major topic for news outlets, while other legislative issues are met with collective yawns in favor of news coverage of various non-political stories such as celebrity or sports news.

A political scientist at the University of California, Davis, Amber Boydstun, laid out a theory that may explain why the Indiana story caught fire in the media. If so, politicians may be able to better miti-gate potential disasters. Political scientists have strived to understand and quantify how the press operates. Boydstun's ideas are laid out in her book, *Making the News: Politics, the Media, and Agenda Setting.* She attempts to show how the daily decisions made in newsrooms produce patterns of operations that can affect national politics in both negative and positive ways.

She observed that the media operates in two distinct modes, one she calls the alarm mode and the other the patrol mode. The latter has been around for years and likens reporters to policemen patrolling their areas, observing what transpires on their streets and alerts the public to any-thing that would affect them. Boydstun stated that, "It's the idea that the press is a watchdog and has a duty and capacity to pay attention to things and let the public know what's going on." However, political sci-entists have largely moved on from this model since it does not account for the large streams of information that newsrooms do not have the resources to cover.

Alarm mode is an idea that has developed over time in political science literature studying congressional oversight. The mode is a reflec-tion of Congress's, and the media's, lack of resources and time to cover every issue and topic occurring in the world. Instead, when disaster strikes or an "alarm" is set off, the media brings the story to the public. However, this model does not completely describe how the media works. It suggests that newsrooms only respond to sensational stories and never dedicate time and resources to provide in-depth coverage and reporting. The model does not account for the investigative reporting that does exist, nor the daily coverage of news that never makes the front page.

According to Boydstun, combining the two modes, patrol and alarm, defines how the media shapes politics in a way either mode could never achieve on its own. Whatever shortcomings one model has the other addresses. The entire process is cyclical and becomes predictable. In the world of politics that can rise and fall in sometimes maddening ways, predictability is invaluable.

The resulting pattern proceeds in the following way. The media dutifully covers the day-to-day stories while operating in patrol mode. Suddenly, a story breaks that requires a newsroom's full attention. Boydstun said in an interview, "Every reporter on a beat is doing patrol-based coverage. But you also get instances where the shock of an alarm draws coverage to a certain area: New Orleans after Katrina, Florida after Trayvon Martin's shooting, healthcare after Obamacare. Now, religious freedom laws in Indiana." These issues all share a common point; they demanded the attention of the public rapidly. The media is then operating in alarm mode. Feedback from the public and politicians heightens the situation and coverage of the event spreads. More resources are poured into reporting on every possible related story and the mode slowly returns to patrol mode as the media keeps a constant watch on new developments. These unique stories caught fire quickly and sustained the public's attention over time.

Boydstun's term for this phenomenon is *sustained media explosion.*" To political scientists, this theory can be put to use by anyone involved with public service. Governor Pence could have predicted the sustainability of Indiana's new legislation to reduce the time devoted to it in the media. Perhaps he could have crafted defending arguments for when the issue did catch fire.

What happened in Indiana is an example of political science in action and in a world where technology can reshape the discussion of politics. When political science got its start with Plato's *Republic*, politics was a discussion reserved for a small group of learned people. Now, anyone with access to the internet and a social media platform has the ability to help shape a debate. Politicians now actively engage with constituents on social media, and people watching political debates are encouraged to comment online with their questions and reactions, shown in a running stream beneath a politician's face in real time.

Though the field of political science remains unchanged at its core, the ability of social media to facilitate the participation of so many people so quickly is changing the way policy is made and makes participation a social event. This is quite a change for a field that was reserved for the erudite as it was in Plato's day.

Over time, political science has evolved naturally. Boydstun's recent work is an extension of the foundation laid by great philosophers of the past. The first elaborate work of European political philosophy is the *Republic* of Plato, a masterpiece of insight and feeling, superbly expressed in dialogue form and probably meant for recitation. Plato's work gave way to many other political scientists and philosophers over time. As the science evolves, it is important to understand the origins and development of political science. This text is broken up into political science's respective fields, and also highlights biographies of some people important to the history of this field.

FIELDS AND SUBFIELDS

Modern university departments of political science (alternatively called government or politics at some institutions) are often divided into several fields, each of which contains various subfields.

- **Domestic politics** is generally the most common field of study; its subfields include public opinion, elections, national government, and state, local, or regional government.
- **Comparative politics** focuses on politics within countries (often grouped into world regions) and analyzes similarities and differences between countries.

- **International relations** considers the political relationships and interactions between countries, including the causes of war, the formation of foreign policy, international political economy, and the structures that increase or decrease the policy options available to governments. International relations is organized as a separate department in some universities.
- **Political theory** includes classical political philosophy and contemporary theoretical perspectives (e.g., constructivism, critical theory, and postmodernism).
- **Public administration** studies the role of the bureaucracy. It is the field most oriented toward practical applications within political science and is often organized as a separate department that prepares students for careers in the civil service.
- **Public law** studies constitutions, legal systems, civil rights, and criminal justice (now increasingly its own discipline).
- **Public policy** examines the passage and implementation of all types of government policies, particularly those related to civil rights, defense, health, education, economic growth, urban renewal, regional development, and environmental protection.

CHAPTER ONE

DEVELOPMENT OF POLITICAL SCIENCE FROM ANCIENT TIMES TO THE EARLY 20TH CENTURY

A lthough political science is a relatively young academic discipline, it has many ancient and early-modern influences.

ANCIENT INFLUENCES

Analyses of politics appeared in ancient cultures in works by various thinkers, including Confucius (551–479 BC) in China and Kautilya (flourished 300 BC) in India. Writings by the historian Ibn Khaldun (1332–1406) in North Africa have greatly influenced the study of politics in the Arabic-speaking world. But the fullest explication of politics has been in the West. Some have identified Plato (428/427–348/347 BC), whose ideal of a stable republic still yields insights and metaphors, as the first political scientist, though most consider Aristotle (384–322 BC), who introduced empirical observation into the study of politics, to be the discipline's true founder.

Aristotle distinguished political systems by the number of persons ruling (one, few, or many) and by whether the form was legitimate (rulers governing in the interests of all) or corrupt (rulers governing in their

1

Bust of Aristotle, Greek philosopher and scientist.

own interests). Legitimate systems included monarchy (rule by one), aristocracy (rule by the few), and polity (rule by the many), while corresponding corrupt forms were tyranny, oligarchy, and democracy. Aristotle considered democracy to be the worst form of government, though in his classification it meant mob rule. The best form of government, a polity, was, in contemporary terms, akin to an efficient, stable democracy. Aristotle's classification endured for centuries and is still helpful in understanding political systems.

Plato and Aristotle focused on perfecting the polis (city-state), a tiny political entity, which for the Greeks meant both society and political system. The conquest of the Mediterranean world and beyond by Aristotle's pupil Alexander the Great (336–323 BC) and, after his death, the division of his empire among his generals brought large new political forms, in which society and political system came to be seen as separate entities. This shift required a new understanding of politics. Hellenistic thinkers asserted the existence of a natural law that applied to all human beings equally; this idea became the foundation of Roman legalism and Christian notions of equality.

Early Christian thinkers, such as St. Augustine (354–430), emphasized the dual loyalty of Christians to both God and temporal rulers, with the clear implication that the "heavenly city" is more important and durable than the earthly one. With this came an otherworldly disdain for politics. For eight centuries knowledge of Aristotle was lost to Europe but preserved by Arab philosophers such as al-Farabi (*c.* 878–*c.* 950) and Averroës (1126–1198). Translations of Aristotle in Spain under the Moors revitalized European thought after about 1200. St. Thomas Aquinas (1224/25–1274) Christianized Aristotle's *Politics* to lend it moral purpose. Aquinas favoured monarchy but despised tyranny, arguing that kingly authority should be limited by law and used for the common good. The Italian poet and philosopher Dante (1265–1321) argued in *De monarchia* (*c.* 1313; *On Monarchy*) for a single world government. At the same time, the philosopher Marsilius of Padua (*c.* 1280–*c.* 1343), in *Defensor Pacis* (1324; "Defender of the Peace"), introduced secularization by elevating the state over the church as the originator of laws. For this, as well as for proposing that legislators be elected, Marsilius ranks as an important modernizer.

EARLY MODERN DEVELOPMENTS

The first modern political scientist was the Italian writer Niccolò Machiavelli (1469–1527). His infamous work *The Prince* (1531) presented amoral advice to actual and would-be princes on the best means of acquiring and holding on to political power. Machiavelli's political philosophy was based on reason rather than religion. Machiavelli believed that Italy could be unified and its foreign occupiers expelled only by ruthless

3

and single-minded princes who rejected any moral constraints on their power. Machiavelli introduced the modern idea of power—how to get it and how to use it—as the crux of politics, a viewpoint shared by today's international relations "realists," rational choice theorists, and others.

The English philosopher Thomas Hobbes (1588–1679) also placed power at the centre of his political analysis. In *Leviathan; or, The Matter, Form, and Power of a Commonwealth, Ecclesiastical and Civil* (1651), completed near the end of the English Civil Wars (1642–51), Hobbes outlined, without reference to an all-powerful God, how humans, endowed with a natural right to self-preservation but living in an anarchic state of nature, would be driven by fear of violent death to form a civil society and submit to a single sovereign authority (a monarch) to ensure their peace and security through a social contract—an actual or hypothetical agreement between citizens and their rulers that defines the rights and duties of each. English philosopher John Locke (1632–1704), who also witnessed the turmoil of an English civil war—the Glorious Revolution (1688–89)—argued in his influential *Two Treatises on Civil Government* (1690) that people form governments through a social contract to preserve their inalienable natural rights to "life, liberty, and property." He further maintained that any government that fails to secure the natural rights of its citizens may properly be overthrown. Locke's views were a powerful force in the intellectual life of 18th-century colonial America and constituted the philosophical basis of the American Declaration of Independence (1776), many of whose drafters, particularly Thomas Jefferson (1743–1826), were well acquainted with Locke's writings.

If Hobbes was the conservative of the "contractualists" and Locke the liberal, then the French philosopher Jean-Jacques Rousseau (1712–78) was the radical. Rousseau's *The Social Contract* (1762) constructs a civil society in which the separate wills of individuals are combined to govern as the "general will" (*volonté générale*) of the collective that overrides individual wills, "forcing a man to be free." Rousseau's radical vision was embraced by French revolutionaries and later by totalitarians, who distorted many of his philosophical lessons.

Montesquieu (1689–1755), a more pragmatic French philosopher, contributed to modern comparative politics with his *The Spirit of Laws* (1748). Montesquieu's sojourn in England convinced him that English liberties were based on the separation and balance of power between Parliament and the monarchy, a principle later embraced by the framers of the Constitution of the United States. Montesquieu also produced an innovative analysis of governance that assigned to each form of government an animating principle—for example, republics are based on virtue, monarchies on honour, and despotisms on fear. Montesquieu's analysis concluded that a country's form of government is determined not by the locus of political power but by how the government enacts public policy.

The Scottish economist and philosopher Adam Smith (1723–90) is considered the founder of classical economic liberalism. In *An Inquiry into the Nature and Causes of the Wealth of Nations* (1776), he argued that the role of the state should be restricted primarily to enforcing contracts in a free market. In contrast, the classical conservatism of the English parliamentarian Edmund Burke (1729–97) maintained that established values and institutions were essential elements of all societies and that revolutions that sought to destroy such values (e.g., the French Revolution) delivered people to irrational impulses and to tyranny. Burke thus introduced an important psychological or cultural insight: that political systems are living organisms that grow over centuries and that depend on a sense of legitimacy that is gradually built up among their subjects.

The early development of political science was also influenced by law. The French political philosopher Jean Bodin (1530–96) articulated a theory of sovereignty that viewed the state as the ultimate source of law in a given territory. Bodin's work, which was undertaken as the modern state was first developing, provided a justification of the legitimacy of national governments, one fiercely defended to this day. Many political scientists, especially in international relations, find Bodin's notion of sovereignty useful for expressing the legitimacy and equality of states.

19TH-CENTURY ROOTS OF CONTEMPORARY POLITICAL SCIENCE

Contemporary political science traces its roots primarily to the 19th century, when the rapid growth of the natural sciences stimulated enthusiasm for the creation of a new social science. Capturing this fervour of scientific optimism was Antoine-Louis-Claude, Comte Destutt de Tracy (1754–1836), who in the 1790s coined the term *idéologie* ("ideology") for his "science of ideas," which, he believed, could perfect society. Also pivotal to the empirical movement was the French utopian socialist Henri de Saint-Simon (1760–1825), a founder of Christian socialism, who in 1813 suggested that morals and politics could become "positive" sciences—that is, disciplines whose authority would rest not upon subjective preconceptions but upon objective evidence. Saint-Simon collaborated with the French mathematician and philosopher Auguste Comte (1798–1857), considered by many to be the founder of sociology, on the publication of the *Plan of the Scientific Operations Necessary for the Reorganization of Society* (1822), which claimed that politics would become a social physics and discover scientific laws of social progress. Although "Comtean positivism," with its enthusiasm for the scientific study of society and its emphasis on using the results of such studies for social improvement, is still very much alive in psychology, contemporary political science shows only traces of Comte's optimism.

The scientific approach to politics developed during the 19th century along two distinct lines that still divide the discipline. In the 1830s the French historian and politician Alexis de Tocqueville (1805–59) brilliantly analyzed democracy in America, concluding that it worked because Americans had developed "the art of association" and were egalitarian group formers. Tocqueville's emphasis on cultural values

A detail of a painting by T. Chassériau showing Alexis de Tocqueville.

contrasted sharply with the views of the German socialist theorists Karl Marx (1818–83) and Friedrich Engels (1820–95), who advanced a materialistic and economic theory of the state as an instrument of domination by the classes that own the means of production. According to Marx and Engels, prevailing values and culture simply reflect the tastes and needs of ruling elites; the state, they charged, is merely "the steering committee of the bourgeoisie." Asserting what they considered to be an immutable scientific law of history, they argued that the state would soon be overthrown by the industrial working class (the proletariat), who would institute socialism, a just and egalitarian form of governance.

The first separate school of political science was established in 1872 in France as the École Libre des Sciences Politiques (now the Institut d'Études Politiques). In 1895 the London School of Economics and Political Science was founded in England, and the first chair of politics was established at the University of Oxford in 1912.

THE EARLY 20TH CENTURY: DEVELOPMENTS IN THE UNITED STATES

Some of the most important developments in political science since it became a distinct academic discipline have occurred in the United States. Politics had long been studied in American universities, but usually as part of the curricula of law, philosophy, or economics. Political science as a separate discipline in universities in the United States dates from 1880, when John W. Burgess, after studying at the École Libre in Paris, established a school of political science at Columbia University in New York City.

Political science in the United States in the last quarter of the 19th century was influenced by the experience of numerous scholars who had done graduate work at German universities, where the discipline was taught as *Staatswissenschaft* ("science of the state") in an ordered, structured, and analytic organization of concepts, definitions, comparisons, and inferences. This highly formalistic and institutional approach, which focused on constitutions, dominated American political science until World War II. The work of American political scientists represented an effort to establish an autonomous discipline, separate from history, moral philosophy, and political economy. Among the new scholars were Woodrow Wilson (1856–1924), who would be elected president of the United States in 1912, and Frank Goodnow, a Columbia University professor of administrative law and, later, president of Johns Hopkins University. Inspired by the work of Charles Darwin (1809–82), Wilson and others led a transformation of American political science from the study of static institutions to the study of social facts, more truly in the positivist temper, less in the analytic tradition, and more oriented toward realism.

Arthur F. Bentley's *The Process of Government*, little noticed at the time of its publication in 1908, greatly influenced the development of political science from the 1930s to the 1950s. Bentley rejected statist abstractions in favour of observable facts and identified groups and their interactions as the basis of political life. Group activity, he argued, determined legislation, administration, and adjudication. In emphasizing behaviour and process, Bentley sounded themes that later became central to political science. In particular, his insistence that "all social movements are brought about by group interaction" is the defining feature of contemporary pluralist and interest-group approaches.

Although Bentley's effort to develop an objective, value-free analysis of politics had no initial consequence, other movements toward this goal enjoyed more immediate success. The principal impetus came from the University of Chicago, where what became known as the Chicago school developed in the mid-1920s and thereafter. The leading figure in this movement was Charles E. Merriam, whose *New Aspects of Politics* (1925) argued for a reconstruction of method in political analysis, urged the greater use of statistics in the aid of empirical observation and measurement, and postulated that "intelligent social control"—a concept reminiscent of the old Comtean positivism—might emerge from the converging interests of politics, medicine, psychiatry, and psychology. An important empirical work of the Chicago school was Merriam and Harold F. Gosnell's *Non-voting, Causes and Methods of Control* (1924), which used sampling methods and survey data and is illustrative of the type of research that came to dominate political science after World War II. Merriam's approach was not entirely new; in 1908 the British political scientist Graham Wallas (1858–1932) had argued in *Human Nature in Politics* that a new political science should favour the quantification of psychological elements (human nature), including nonrational and subconscious inferences, a view similarly expressed in *Public Opinion* (1922) by the American journalist and political scientist Walter Lippmann (1889–1974).

Harold Lasswell (1902–78), a member of the Chicago group, carried the psychological approach to Yale University, where he had a commanding influence. His *Psychopathology and Politics* (1930) and *Power and Personality* (1948) fused categories of Freudian psychology with considerations of power. Many political scientists attempted to use Freudian psychology to analyze politics, but none succeeded in establishing it as a firm basis of political science, because it depended too much on subjective insights and often could not be verified empirically.

Merriam's *Political Power* (1934) and Lasswell's classic *Politics: Who Gets What, When, How* (1936)—the title of which articulated the basic definition of politics—gave a central place to the phenomenon of power in the empirical study of politics. Merriam discussed how power comes into being, how it becomes "authority" (which he equated with power), the techniques of power holders, the defenses of those over whom power is wielded, and the dissipation of power. Lasswell focused on "influence and the influential," laying the basis for subsequent "elite" theories of politics. Although the various members of the Chicago school ostensibly sought to develop political science as a value-free discipline, it had two central predilections: it accepted democratic values, and it attempted to improve the operation of democratic systems. Power approaches also became central in the burgeoning field of international relations, particularly after World War II. Hans Morgenthau (1904–80), a German refugee and analyst of world politics, argued succinctly in *Politics Among Nations* (1948) that "all politics is a struggle for power."

The totalitarian dictatorships that developed in Europe and Asia in the 1920s and '30s and the onset of World War II turned political science, particularly in the United States, away from its focus on institutions, law, and procedures. The constitution of Germany's post-World War I Weimar Republic had been an excellent model, but it failed in practice because too few Germans were then committed supporters of democracy. Likewise, the Soviet Union's 1936 constitution appeared democratic but in reality was merely an attempt to mask the brutal dictatorship of Joseph Stalin. Works of this period focused on the role of elites, political parties, and interest groups, on legislative and bureaucratic processes, and especially on how voters in democracies make their electoral choices. This new interest in actual political behaviour became known as "behavioralism." The result was that much of political science became political sociology.

THE EARLY 20TH CENTURY: DEVELOPMENTS OUTSIDE THE UNITED STATES

Since the time of Marx and Engels, political scientists have continued to debate the relative importance of culture and economic structures in determining human behaviour and the organization of society. In the late 19th and early 20th centuries, the Italian economists Gaetano Mosca (1858–1941) and Vilfredo Pareto (1848–1923) echoed Marx's analysis that society was ruled by elites, but they considered this both permanent and natural. They were joined by the German-born Italian political sociologist and economist Robert Michels (1876–1936), whose "iron law of oligarchy" declared rule by the few to be inevitable. Mosca, Pareto, and Michels all agreed that the overthrow of the existing "political class" would simply result in its replacement by another, a view that was supported in the mid-20th century by Yugoslav dissident Milovan Djilas (1911–95) in his *The New Class* (1957). Pareto also contributed the idea (which he borrowed from economics) that society is a system tending toward equilibrium: like an economic system, a society that becomes out of balance will tend to correct itself by developing new institutions and laws or by redistributing power. This approach was adopted by much of academic political science after World War II and was later developed by "systems" theory.

In the early 20th century, the Swedish political scientist Rudolf Kjellén (1864–1922) treated the state as a fusion of organic and cultural elements determined by geography. Kjellén is credited with coining the term *geopolitics (geopolitik)*, which acquired a sinister connotation in the years after World War I, when German expansionists appealed to geopolitical arguments in support of the Nazi regime of Adolf Hitler. Although geopolitics still exerts a considerable influence on political science, particularly in the areas of international relations and foreign policy, the discipline of political geography developed into a distinct subfield of geography rather than of political science.

The German sociologist Max Weber (1864–1920), who rejected Marx and embraced Tocqueville's emphasis on culture and values, was perhaps the most influential figure in political science in the late 19th and early 20th centuries. Weber claimed that Protestantism triggered capitalism: the Calvinist idea of predestination led individuals to try to prove, by amassing capital, that they were predestined for heaven. Weber's theory of the Protestant ethic is still disputed, but not the fact that religion and culture powerfully influence economic and political development.

OTHER POLITICAL SCIENCE SCHOLARS

In *The English Constitution* (1867), the English economist and political analyst Walter Bagehot (1826–77), who was also an editor of *The Economist*, famously distinguished between Britain's "dignified" offices (e.g., the monarch) and its "efficient" offices (e.g., the prime minister). James Bryce (1838–1922), who taught civil law at the University of Oxford, produced one of the earliest and most influential studies of the U.S. political system in *The American Commonwealth* (1888). The Belorussian political scientist Moisey Ostrogorsky (1854–1919), who was educated at the École Libre des Sciences Politiques in Paris, pioneered the study of parties, elections, and public opinion in *Democracy and the Organization of Political Parties* (originally written in French; 1902), which focused on the United States and Britain. In Paris, André Siegfried, teaching at the École Libre des Sciences Politiques and the Collège de France, introduced the use of maps to demonstrate the influence of geography on politics. At first few Britons turned to behavioralism and quantification, instead continuing in their inclination toward political philosophy. In contrast, the Swedish scholar Herbert Tingsten (1896–1973), in his seminal *Political Behaviour: Studies in Election Statistics* (1937), developed the connections between social groups and their voting tendencies. Before World War II the large areas of the world that were colonies or dictatorships made few important contributions to the growth of political science.

Early 20th century German political economist and social scientist Max Weber (1864–1920).

Weber understood that the social sciences could not simply mimic the natural sciences, because humans attach widely varying meanings and loyalties to their leaders and institutions. It is not simply facts that matter but how people perceive, interpret, and react to these facts; this makes causality in the social sciences far more complex than in the natural sciences. To be objective, therefore, the social scientist must take into account human subjectivity.

Weber discerned three types of authority: traditional (as in monarchies), charismatic (a concept he developed to refer to the personal drawing power of revolutionary leaders), and rational-legal (characteristic of modern societies). Weber coined the term *bureaucracy*, and he was the first to study bureaucracies systematically. His theories, which focused on culture as a chief source of economic growth and democracy, still find support among contemporary political scientists, and he must be ranked equally as one of the founders of both modern sociology and modern political science.

CHAPTER TWO

POST-WORLD WAR II TRENDS IN POLITICAL SCIENCE

Perhaps the most important irreversible change in political science after World War II was that the scope of the discipline was expanded to include the study of politics in Asia, Africa, and Latin America—areas that had been largely ignored in favour of Europe and North America. This trend was encouraged by the Cold War competition between the United States and the Soviet Union for influence over the political development of newly independent countries. The scholarship produced in these countries, however, remained largely derivative of developments in Europe and the United States. Researchers in Asia, Africa, and Latin America, often in partnership with European and American colleagues, produced significant studies on decolonization, ideology, federalism, corruption, and political instability. In Latin America a Marxist-oriented view called dependency theory was popular from the 1960s to the '80s. Greatly influencing the study of international relations in the United States and Europe as well as in developing countries, dependency theorists argued that Latin America's problems were rooted in its subservient economic and political relationship to the United States and Western Europe. More recently, Latin American political scientists, influenced by methods developed in American universities, undertook empirical studies of the sources of democracy and instability, such as Arturo Valenzuela's *The Breakdown of Democratic Regimes* (1978). African, Asian, and Latin American

Che Guevera (above) was a leading theoretician and tactician of guerrilla warfare and a prominent figure in Fidel Castro's Communist revolution in Cuba (1956–59).

political scientists also made important contributions as teachers on the faculties of American and European universities.

Outside the United States, where political science initially was less quantitative, there were several outstanding works. Like Lasswell, the German philosopher Theodor Adorno (1903–69) and others adopted Freudian insights in their pioneering study *The Authoritarian Personality* (1950), which used a 29-item questionnaire to detect the susceptibility of individuals to fascist beliefs. The French political scientist Maurice Duverger's *Political Parties* (1951) is still highly regarded, not only for its classification of parties but also for its linking of party systems with electoral systems. Duverger argued that single-member-district electoral systems that require only a plurality to win election tend to produce two-party systems, whereas proportional-representation systems tend to produce multiparty systems; this generalization was later called "Duverger's law." The French sociologist Michel Crozier's *The Bureaucratic Phenomenon* (1964) found that Weber's idealized bureaucracy is quite messy, political, and varied. Each bureaucracy is a political subculture; what is rational and routine in one bureau may be quite different in another. Crozier thus influenced the subsequent "bureaucratic politics" approach of the 1970s.

BEHAVIORALISM

Behavioralism, which was one of the dominant approaches in the 1950s and '60s, is the view that the subject matter of political science should be limited to phenomena that are independently observable and quantifiable. It assumes that political institutions largely reflect underlying social forces and that the study of politics should begin with society, culture, and public opinion. To this end, behavioralists utilize the methodology of the social sciences—primarily psychology—to establish statistical relationships between independent variables (presumed causes) and dependent variables (presumed effects). For example, a behavioralist might use detailed election data to argue that voters in rural areas tend to vote for candidates who are more conservative, while voters in cities generally favour candidates who are more liberal. The prominence of behavioralists in the post-World War II period helped to lead political science in a much more scientific direction. For many behavioralists, only such quantified studies can be considered political science in the strict sense; they often contrasted their studies with those of the so-called traditionalists, who attempted to explain politics by using unquantified descriptions, anecdotes, historical analogies, ideologies, and philosophy. Like behaviourism in psychology, behavioralism in political science attempted to discard intuition, or at least to support it with empirical observation. A traditionalist, in contrast, might attempt to support intuition with reason alone.

Perhaps the most important behavioral contributions to political science were election studies. In 1955 American political scientist V.O. Key, Jr. (1908–63), identified as "critical," or "realigning," several elections in which American voters shifted their long-term party affiliation massively from one political party to another, giving rise to the dominance of the Republican Party from 1860 to 1932 and of the Democratic Party after 1932. Pioneering statistical electoral analyses were conducted by the University of Michigan's Survey Research Center (SRC), which was developed in the 1940s. In *The American Voter* (1960), Angus Campbell, Philip Converse, William Miller, and Donald Stokes used the results of studies by the SRC to develop the concept of party identification—the long-term psychological attachment of a voter to a political party. The long-recognized influences of religion, social class, region, and ethnicity, they argued, contribute to voting behaviour only insofar as the voter has been socialized, primarily by parents, to adopt a particular party identification.

Behavioral approaches were soon adopted outside the United States, often by scholars with connections to American universities. The University of Oxford initiated election studies in the 1960s, and David Butler and Donald Stokes—one of the authors of *The American*

Voter—adapted much of the American study in *Political Change in Britain: Forces Shaping Electoral Choice* (1969). They found that political generation (the era in which one was born) and "duration of partisanship" also predict party identification—that is, the length of time one has been a partisan heavily predicts one's vote. They also found that party identification, initially transmitted by one's parents, may change under the impact of historic events. The influential Norwegian scholar Stein Rokkan pioneered the use of cross-national quantitative data to examine the interaction of party systems and social divisions based on class, religion, and region, which in combination explain much voting behaviour. Rokkan identified the importance of "centre-periphery" tensions, finding that outlying regions of a country tend to vote differently from the area where political and economic activities are centred. The extensive Eurobarometer series—public-opinion surveys carried out in European Union countries since 1973 on behalf of the European Commission—have given European behavioralists a solid statistical base on a range of political, social, economic, and cultural issues; the surveys have provided valuable data for examining trends over time, and they have shown, among other things, that modern European ideological opinion clusters around the political centre, suggesting that stable democratic systems have taken root. More recently, Transparency International, founded in 1993 in Berlin, has conducted worldwide surveys that attempt to quantify corruption. In Latin America, Guillermo O'Donnell and Arturo Valenzuela used public-opinion surveys and voting, economic, and demographic data to examine the forces that have destabilized democracy there.

Though behavioral research yielded important insights into the political behaviour of individuals, it often explained little about actual governance. Voting studies, for example, rarely provided an understanding of public policy. Because behavioral research tended to be limited to topics that were amenable to quantitative study, it was often dismissed as narrow and irrelevant to major political issues. Indeed, intense methodological debates among behavioralists (and within the discipline more broadly) often seemed arcane, filled with esoteric jargon and addressed to issues of little concern to most citizens. Because behavioralists needed quantitative survey and electoral data, which were often unavailable in dictatorships or less-affluent countries, their approach was useless in many parts of the world. In addition, the reliability of behavioral research was called into question by its dependence in large part on verbal responses to questionnaires. Analyses of survey results have shown that respondents often give socially desirable answers and are likely to conceal their true feelings on controversial topics; moreover, the wording of questions, as well as the ordering of possible answers, can affect the results, making concrete conclusions difficult. Finally, many behavioral findings revealed nothing new but simply restated well-established or obvious conclusions, such as the observation that wealthy people tend to vote conservative and

Arturo Valenzuela, author of *The Breakdown of Democratic Regimes.*

poor and working-class people tend to vote liberal or left-of-centre. For all of these reasons, behavioralism did not become the sole methodology in political science, and many behavioralists eventually acknowledged the need for the unquantified insights of traditionalists; by the late 1960s political scientists called this the "postbehavioral synthesis."

THE EUROBAROMERTER

This is a series of surveys initiated by the European Commission, the executive arm of what is now the European Union (EU), to measure public opinion in its member states. The Eurobarometer was created in 1973, when the European Parliament released a report requesting the establishment of a permanent research institute that would study European public opinion. After pilot studies were completed, the first official Eurobarometer survey was conducted in 1974, and its results were released later that year.

The first study was designed by the first Eurobarometer director, Jacques-René Rabier, and was conducted in the nine countries—France, West Germany, the United Kingdom, Italy, the Netherlands, Belgium, Denmark, Ireland, and Luxembourg—that were then the members of the European Economic Community (EEC), a precursor to the EU. Over time the Eurobarometer grew from surveying the nine original countries to include new members of the EEC and its successors, the European Community and EU.

Eurobarometer surveys allow for monitoring the evolution of public opinion in the EU member states, which helps the European Commission with decision making and in the evaluation of its work. Eurobarometer data are also often cited by mass media and are used by research scholars in communication, public opinion, and political science.

POLITICAL CULTURE

Political culture may be defined as the political psychology of a country or nation (or subgroup thereof). Political culture studies attempt to uncover deep-seated, long-held values characteristic of a society or group rather than ephemeral attitudes toward specific issues that might be gathered through public-opinion surveys. Several major studies using a political culture approach appeared simultaneously with the behavioral studies of the late 1950s, adding psychological and anthropological insights to statistical covariance. The study of political culture was hardly new; since at least the time of Plato, virtually all political thinkers have acknowledged the importance of what Tocqueville called "habits of the heart" in making the political system work as it does. Modern political culture approaches were motivated in part by a desire to understand the rise of totalitarian regimes in the 20th century in Russia, Germany, and Italy, and many early studies focused on Nazi Germany; one early political culture study, Edward Banfield's *The Moral Basis of a Backward Society* (1958), argued that poverty in southern Italy grew out of a psychological inability to trust or to form associations beyond the immediate family, a finding that was long controversial but is now accepted by many.

Perhaps the most important work of political culture was Gabriel Almond and Sidney Verba's *The Civic Culture: Political Attitudes and Democracy in Five Nations* (1963), which surveyed 1,000-person samples in the United States, the United Kingdom, Germany, Italy, and Mexico. Almond and Verba identified three types of political culture: (1) participant, in which citizens understand and take part in politics and voluntary associations, (2) subject, in which citizens largely obey but participate little, and (3) parochial, in which citizens have neither knowledge of nor interest in politics. The authors found that democratic stability arises from a balance or mixture of these cultures, a conclusion similar to that drawn by Aristotle. In Almond and Verba's edited volume *The Civic Culture Revisited* (1980), several authors demonstrated

23

that political culture in each of their subject countries was undergoing major change, little of which was predictable from the original study, suggesting that political culture, while more durable than mere public opinion, is never static. Critics of *The Civic Culture* also pointed out that political structures can affect culture. The effective governance and economic policies of West Germany's government made that country's citizens embrace democracy, whereas Britain's economic decline made Britons more cynical about politics. The problem, again, is determining causality.

Over the decades Seymour Lipset, who served as president of both the American Sociological Association and the American Political Science Association, turned from explanations of political values based on social class to those based on history and culture, which, he argued, displayed consistency throughout history. American political scientist Robert Putnam followed in this Tocquevillian tradition in *Making Democracy Work: Civic Traditions in Modern Italy* (1993), which demonstrated that the historical cultures of Italy's regions explain their current political situations. In *Bowling Alone: The Collapse and Revival of American Community* (2000), Putnam claimed that the American tendency to form citizen groups, a characteristic that Tocqueville praised, was weakening. Americans were less often joining groups and participating in politics, Putnam argued, leading to a loss of "social capital" (the collective value of social networks) and potentially undermining democracy, a worry shared by other political observers in the United States.

Adopting what became known as the "path-dependent development" approach, advocates of the historical-cultural school maintained that contemporary society is a reflection of society in ages past. The political culture approach declined in the 1970s but was later revived as political scientists incorporated it into explanations of why some countries experienced economic growth and established democratic political systems while others did not. Some suggested that the rapid economic growth and democratization that took place in some East Asian countries in the second half of the 20th century was facilitated by a political culture based on Confucianism. In Africa and Latin America, they argued, the absence of a culture that valued hard work and capital accumulation led to the stagnation of much of those regions.

SYSTEMS ANALYSIS

Systems analysis, which was influenced by the Austrian Canadian biologist Ludwig von Bertalanffy and the American sociologist Talcott Parsons (1902–79), is a broad descriptive theory of how the various parts and levels of a political system interact with each other. The central idea of systems analysis is based on an analogy with biology: just as the heart, lungs, and blood function as a whole, so do the components of social and political systems. When one component changes or comes under stress, the other components will adjust to compensate.

Systems analysis studies first appeared alongside behavioral and political culture studies in the 1950s. A groundbreaking work employing the approach, David Easton's *The Political System* (1953), conceived the political system as integrating all activities through which social policy is formulated and executed—that is, the political system is the policy-making process. Easton defined political behaviour as the "authoritative allocation of values," or the distribution of rewards in wealth, power, and status that the system may provide. In doing so, he distinguished his sense of the subject matter of political science from that of Lasswell, who had argued that political science is concerned with the distribution and content of patterns of value throughout society. Easton's conception of system emphasizes linkages between the system and its environment. Inputs (demands) flow into the system and are converted into outputs (decisions and actions) that constitute the authoritative allocation of values. Drawing on cybernetics, the Czech-born American political scientist Karl Deutsch used a systems perspective to view the political system as a communications network. Following Deutsch, some political scientists tried briefly to establish communications as the basis of politics.

Systems analysis was applied to international relations to explain how the forces of the international system affect the behaviour of states. The American political scientist Morton Kaplan delineated types of international systems and their logical consequences in *System and Process in International Politics* (1957). According to Kaplan, for example, the Cold War rivalry between the United States and the Soviet Union brought about a bipolar international system that governed much of the two countries' foreign and security policies.

By the 1970s, systems approaches to domestic politics were criticized and generally abandoned as unverifiable abstractions of little explanatory or predictive power. (In international politics, however, systems approaches remained important.) On closer examination, the "conversion process" of systems theory—i.e., the transformation of inputs into outputs—struck many as simply plain old "politics." Another problem was that much of systems theory took as its norm and model an idealized version of American politics that did not apply universally to the domestic politics of all societies. Systems analysis also was unable to explain certain policy decisions that were made despite the absence of predominating favourable inputs, such as the decision by U.S. Pres. Lyndon B. Johnson to deepen U.S. involvement in the war in Vietnam. Finally, systems theorists unrealistically reified the systems of the countries they studied, portraying them as durable and stable because they were supposed to correct and reform themselves. They were thus unable to explain defective systems or systemic upheavals, such as the collapse of communist regimes in eastern and central Europe in 1989–91.

There was no consensus among political scientists concerning the system that developed after the end of the Cold War. Some scholars believed that there was a return to a 19th-century balance-of-power system, in which multiple states make and remake alliances. Others argued for the existence of a multipolar system consisting of trade blocs that were neither mutually hostile nor totally cooperative with each other. Some argued that the international system became unipolar, the United States being the single dominant world power. The American political

26

scientist Samuel Huntington, in a controversial article published in 1993 and a book, *The Clash of Civilizations and the Remaking of World Order*, published in 1996, used cultural theory to propose that the emerging international system constituted a "clash of civilizations." Several civilizations, each based mostly on religion, variously clashed and cooperated. The worst clashes, he argued, took place between Islamic and other civilizations. Many scholars rejected Huntington's analysis as simplistic and ill-informed, but others found it persuasive, especially after the September 11 attacks of 2001 and subsequent U.S. military attacks.

THEORY OF RATIONAL CHOICE

The dominant school of thought in political science in the late 20th century was rational choice theory. For rational choice theorists, history and culture are irrelevant to understanding political behaviour; instead, it is sufficient to know the actors' interests and to assume that they pursue them rationally. Whereas the earlier decision-making approach sought to explain the decisions of elite groups (mostly in matters of foreign policy), rational choice theorists attempted to apply their far more formal theory (which sometimes involved the use of mathematical notation) to all facets of political life. Many believed they had found the key that would at last make political science truly scientific. In *An Economic Theory of Democracy* (1957), an early work in rational choice theory, Anthony Downs claimed that significant elements of political life could be explained in terms of voter self-interest. Downs showed that in democracies the aggregate distribution of political opinion forms a bell-shaped curve, with most voters possessing moderate opinions; he argued that this fact forces political parties in democracies to adopt centrist positions. The founder of rational choice theory was William Riker, who applied economic and game-theoretic approaches to develop increasingly complex mathematical models of politics. In *The*

Theory of Political Coalitions (1962), Riker demonstrated by mathematical reasoning why and how politicians form alliances. Riker and his followers applied this version of rational choice theory—which they variously called rational choice, public choice, social choice, formal modeling, or positive political theory—to explain almost everything, including voting, legislation, wars, and bureaucracy. Some researchers used games to reproduce key decisions in small-group experiments.

Rational choice theory identified—or rediscovered—at least two major explanatory factors that some political scientists had neglected: (1) that politicians are endlessly opportunistic and (2) that all decisions take place in some type of institutional setting. Rational choice theorists argued that political institutions structure the opportunities available to politicians and thus help to explain their actions.

By the early 21st century, rational choice theory was being stiffly challenged. Critics alleged that it simply mathematized the obvious and, in searching for universal patterns, ignored important cultural contexts, which thus rendered it unable to predict much of importance; another charge was that the choices the theory sought to explain appeared "rational" only in retrospect. Reacting to such criticisms, some rational choice theorists began calling themselves "new institutionalists" or "structuralists" to emphasize their view that all political choices take place within specific institutional structures. U.S. congressmen, for example, typically calculate how their votes on bills will help or hurt their chances for reelection. In this way, rational choice theory led political science back to its traditional concern with political institutions, such as parliaments and laws. In more recent years, increasing numbers of rational choice theorists have backed away from claims that their approach is capable of explaining every political phenomenon.

DEMOCRATIC THEORY

Late in the 20th century, some political scientists returned to the question of how to achieve the good, just, and stable polity—that is, by returning to the study of democracy. Although the approaches taken were highly diverse, most researchers attempted to identify the factors by which democracies are established and sustained. Democratic theory was revived in earnest in the late 1980s, when communist regimes were collapsing throughout Eastern Europe, and was accompanied by the founding of the influential *Journal of Democracy* in 1990.

The American political theorist Robert Dahl, who had long been a scholar of the topic, viewed democracy as the pluralist interplay of groups in what he called a "polyarchy." Historical-cultural thinkers such as Lipset traced the origins of democracy to the values that democratic societies developed long ago. Samuel Huntington, perhaps the most influential post-World War II American political scientist, worried about a "democratic distemper" in which citizens demand more than the system can deliver. Huntington also viewed democracy as coming in waves—the most recent having started in 1974 in Greece and Portugal and having subsequently washed over Spain and Latin America—but warned of a potential reverse wave toward authoritarianism. The Spanish American political scientist Juan Linz explored how democracies can decline, and the Dutch-born American scholar Arend Lijphart considered the institutional arrangements (political parties and electoral systems, executives and parliaments) that were most likely to produce stable political systems.

Modernization theorists noted the connection between democracy and economic development but were unable to determine whether economic development typically precedes democracy or vice versa. Few of them regarded democracy as inevitable, and many noted its philosophical, psychological, and social prerequisites, suggesting that democracy may be a largely Western phenomenon that is not easily transplanted to non-Western cultures. Others, however, argued that democracy is a universal value that transcends culture. Some worried that the legitimacy of established democracies was eroding in the late 20th and early 21st centuries, as citizens became disenchanted with the political process and many moved away from political participation in favour of private pursuits. Voter turnout fell in most countries, in part because citizens saw little difference between the major political parties, believing them to be essentially power-seeking and self-serving. Some blamed the media for focusing on political scandals instead of issues of substance. Nevertheless, some scholars argued that citizens were generally better-educated and more critical than they were given credit for.

CHAPTER THREE

INTERNATIONAL RELATIONS

The branch of political science that studies the relations of nation states with each other and with international organizations is called international relations.

HISTORICAL DEVELOPMENT

The field of international relations emerged at the beginning of the 20th century largely in the West and in particular in the United States as that country grew in power and influence. Whereas the study of international relations in the newly founded Soviet Union and later in communist China was stultified by officially imposed Marxist ideology, in the West the field flourished as the result of a number of factors: a growing demand to find less-dangerous and more-effective means of conducting relations between peoples, societies, governments, and economies; a surge of writing and research inspired by the belief that systematic observation and inquiry could dispel ignorance and serve human betterment; and the popularization of political affairs, including foreign affairs. This increasing popularization of international relations reinforced the idea that general education should include instruction in foreign affairs and that knowledge should be advanced in the interests of greater public control and oversight of foreign and military policy.

This new perspective was articulated by U.S. Pres. Woodrow Wilson in his program for relations between the Great Powers following a settlement of World War I. The first of his Fourteen Points, as his program

British troops during World War I in a trench along the Western Front.

came to be known, was a call for "open covenants of peace, openly arrived at" in place of the secret treaties that were believed to have contributed to the outbreak of the war. The extreme devastation caused by the war strengthened the conviction among political leaders that not enough was known about international relations and that universities should promote research and teaching on issues related to international cooperation and war and peace.

International relations scholarship prior to World War I was conducted primarily in two loosely organized branches of learning: diplomatic history and international law. Involving meticulous archival and other primary-source research, diplomatic history emphasized the uniqueness of international events and the methods of diplomacy as it was actually conducted. International law—especially the law of war—had a long history in international relations and was viewed as the source of fundamental normative standards of international conduct. The emergence of international relations was to broaden the scope of international law beyond this traditional focal point.

BETWEEN THE TWO WORLD WARS

During the 1920s new centres, institutes, schools, and university departments devoted to teaching and research in international relations were created in Europe and North America. In addition, private organizations promoting the study of international relations were formed, and substantial philanthropic grants were made to support scholarly journals, to sponsor training institutes, conferences, and seminars, and to stimulate university research.

Three subject areas initially commanded the most attention, each having its roots in World War I. During the revolutionary upheavals at the end of the war, major portions of the government archives of imperial Russia and imperial Germany were opened, making possible some impressive scholarly work in diplomatic history that pieced together the unknown history of prewar alliances, secret diplomacy, and military planning. These materials were integrated to provide detailed explanations of the origins of World War I.

The newly created League of Nations also captured significant attention. Some of the international relations schools that were founded in the interwar period were explicitly created to prepare civil servants for what was expected to be the dawning age of international government. Accordingly, intensive study was devoted to the genesis and organization of the league, the history of earlier plans for international federations,

Henry Kissinger served as secretary of state under U.S. presidents Nixon and Ford.

and the analysis of the problems and procedures of international organization and international law.

The third focal point of international relations scholarship was an offshoot of the peace movement and was concerned primarily with understanding the causes and costs of war, as well as its political, sociological, economic, and psychological dimensions.

In the 1930s the breakdown of the League of Nations, the rise of aggressive dictatorships in Italy, Germany, and Japan, and the onset of World War II produced a strong reaction against international government and against peace-inspired topics in the study of international relations. The moral idealism inherent in these topics was criticized as unrealistic and impractical, and the academic study of international relations came to be regarded as the handiwork of starry-eyed peace visionaries who ignored the hard facts of international politics. As the desired world of peaceful conflict resolution and adherence to international law grew more distant from the existing world of aggressive dictatorships, a new approach to the study of international relations, known as realism, increasingly dominated the field. Some topics of study in international relations that are still considered novel or of recent origin were already being vigorously explored in the interwar period. The scholarly contributions of some individuals in the 1930s were particularly noteworthy because they foreshadowed the development of international relations studies after World War II.

The broadened definition and scope of the study of international relations were among the fundamental contributions of scholars of the interwar period. Many of these innovators were enlisted by governments during World War II for work in intelligence and propaganda, as well as other aspects of wartime planning. In this respect the war stimulated systematic social-scientific investigations of international phenomena. It also led to important technological advances—notably the computer— that would later have a major impact on the study of international relations.

In other ways World War II was a divide for academic international relations. The war itself brought about a drastic change in the agenda of world politics, and the postwar intellectual climate was characterized by a marked shift away from many earlier interests, emphases, and problems. New security issues emerged, including the issue of nuclear weapons, which led to extensive writings on deterrence as a basis of strategic stability. Bernard Brodie's treatise on nuclear deterrence was highly influential, as was the work of Herman Kahn, Glenn Snyder, Thomas C. Schelling, Henry A. Kissinger, and Albert Wohlstetter. Other issues that were addressed in the vast literature of international relations include international, and especially European, integration; alliances and alignment, such as the North Atlantic Treaty Organization (NATO); ideologies; foreign-policy decision making; theories about conflict and war; the study of low-intensity conflict; crisis management; international organizations; and the foreign policies of the increasing number of states that became part of the international system in the mid- to late 20th century.

NATO

This military alliance established by the North Atlantic Treaty (also called the Washington Treaty) of April 4, 1949, sought to create a counterweight to Soviet armies stationed in central and eastern Europe after World War II. Its original members were Belgium, Canada, Denmark, France, Iceland, Italy, Luxembourg, the Netherlands, Norway, Portugal, the United Kingdom, and the United States. Joining the original signatories were Greece and Turkey (1952); West Germany (1955; from 1990 as Germany); Spain (1982); the Czech Republic, Hungary, and Poland (1999); Bulgaria, Estonia, Latvia, Lithuania, Romania, Slovakia, and Slovenia (2004); and Albania and Croatia (2009). France withdrew from the integrated military command of NATO in 1966 but remained a member of the organization; it resumed its position in NATO's military command in 2009.

The heart of NATO is expressed in Article 5 of the North Atlantic Treaty, in which the signatory members agree that "an armed attack against one or more of them in Europe or North America shall be considered an attack against them all; and consequently they agree that, if such an armed attack occurs, each of them, in exercise of the right of individual or collective self-defense recognized by Article 51 of the Charter of the United Nations, will assist the Party or Parties so attacked by taking forthwith, individually and in concert with the other Parties, such action as it deems necessary, including the use of armed force, to restore and maintain the security of the North Atlantic area."

THE POSTWAR ASCENDANCY OF REALISM

Hans J. Morgenthau's *Politics Among Nations* (1948) helped to meet the need for a general theoretical framework. Not only did it become one of the most extensively used textbooks in the United States and Britain—it continued to be republished over the next half century—it also was an essential exposition of the realist theory of international relations. Numerous other contributors to realist theory emerged in the decade or so after World War II, including Arnold Wolfers, George F. Kennan, Robert Strausz-Hupé, Kissinger, and the theologian Reinhold Niebuhr.

Although there are many variations of realism, all of them make use of the core concepts of national interest and the struggle for power. According to realism, states exist within an anarchic international system in which they are ultimately dependent on their own capabilities, or power, to further their national interests. The most important national interest is the survival of the state, including its people, political system, and territorial integrity. Other major interests for realists include preservation of the culture and the economy. Realists contend that, as long as the world is divided into nation-states in an anarchic setting, national interest will remain the essence of international politics. The struggle for power is part of human nature and takes essentially two forms: collaboration and competition. Collaboration occurs when parties find that their interests coincide (e.g., when they form alliances or coalitions designed to maximize their collective power, usually against an adversary). Rivalry, competition, and conflict result from the clash of national interests that is characteristic of the anarchic system. Accommodation between states is possible through skillful political leadership, which includes the prioritizing of national goals in order to limit conflicts with other states.

In an international system composed of sovereign states, the survival of both the states and the system depends on the intelligent pursuit

American political sociologist Seymour Martin Lipset (1922–2006.)

of national interests and the accurate calculation of national power. Realists caution that messianic religious and ideological crusades can obscure core national interests and threaten the survival of individual states and the international system itself. Such crusades included, for Morgenthau, the pursuit of global communism or global democracy, each of which would inevitably clash with the other or with other competing ideologies. The attempt to reform countries toward the ideal of universal trust and cooperation, according to realists, runs counter to human nature, which is inclined toward competition, conflict, and war.

THE BEHAVIORAL APPROACH AND THE TASK OF INTEGRATION

The 1950s marked the emergence of behavioral theory, which emphasized narrowly focused quantitative studies designed to obtain precise results. Because of the great number of new topics investigated at the time, much of the intellectual effort of the mid-1950s to mid-1960s—the so-called "behavioral decade"—went into the task of comparing, interpreting, and integrating various concepts from new areas of study.

The scholarly goal of the period was to link theories, or to connect so-called "islands of theory," into a greater, more comprehensive theory of international relations.

The general attitude of the behavioral decade was that the facts of international relations are multidimensional and therefore have multiple causes. This conclusion supported, and in turn was supported by, the related view that an adequate account of these facts could not be provided in a single integrated theory and that multiple separate theories were required instead. By the 1960s, for example, studies of international conflict had come to encompass a number of different perspectives, including the realist theory of the struggle for power between states and the Marxist notion of global class conflict, as well as other explanations. At the same time, conflict theory coexisted with economic and political integration theory and game theory, each of which approached the phenomena of international conflict from a distinct perspective.

By the end of the behavioral decade there was a growing consensus that the study of international relations should encompass both quantitative and qualitative analyses. Whereas quantitative methodologies were recognized as useful for measuring and comparing international phenomena and identifying common features and patterns of behaviour, qualitative analyses, by focusing on one case or a comparison of cases involving specific research questions, hypotheses, or categories, were thought to provide a deeper understanding of what is unique about political leaders, nations, and important international events such as World War II and the Cold War.

THE LATER 20TH CENTURY

The influence of behaviourism helped to organize the various theories of international relations and the discipline into essentially two principal parts, or perspectives: the foreign-policy perspective and the international-system-analysis perspective.

FOREIGN POLICY AND INTERNATIONAL SYSTEMS

Within each of these perspectives there developed various theories. The foreign-policy perspective, for example, encompasses theories about the behaviour of individual states or categories of states such as democracies or totalitarian dictatorships, and the international-system-analysis perspective encompasses theories of the interactions between states and how the number of states and their respective capabilities affect their relations with each other. The foreign-policy perspective also includes studies of the traits, structures, or processes within a national society or polity that determine or influence how that society or polity participates in international relations. One such study, known as the decision-making approach, analyzes the information that decision makers use, their perceptions and motivations, the influence on their behaviour of public opinion, the organizational settings in which they operate, and their intellectual, cultural, and societal backgrounds. Studies that analyze the relations between the wealth, power, or technological level of a state and its international status and role provide other illustrations of the foreign-policy perspective.

Comparative foreign-policy analysis first appeared during the mid-1960s. By comparing the domestic sources of external conduct in different countries, using standard criteria of data selection and analysis, this approach seeks to develop generalized accounts of foreign-policy performance, including theories that explore the relationship between the type of domestic-external linkage a country displays and its political and economic system and level of social development. Some research also has explored the extent to which certain patterns of behaviour, such as violent demonstrations or protests, may spread from one state to another.

Whereas foreign-policy analysis concentrates on the units of the international system, international-system analysis is concerned with the structure of the system, the interactions between its units, and the implications for peace and war, or cooperation and conflict, of the existence of different types of states. The term *interactions* suggests challenge and response, give and take, move and countermove, or inputs and outputs. Diplomatic histories feature narratives of action and response in international situations and attempt to interpret the meanings of the exchanges. Balance-of-power theory, which asserts that states act to protect themselves by forming alliances against powerful states or coalitions of states, is another example of the international-system perspective. Still other examples include explanations and descriptions of bargaining in international negotiations and studies of arms races and other escalating action-reaction processes.

THE GENERAL-SYSTEM PERSPECTIVE

The so-called general-system perspective on international relations, which attempts to develop a comprehensive understanding of the dynamics of the relations between states, may be compared to the map of a little-explored continent. Outlines, broad features, and a continental delineation are not in question, but everything else remains in doubt, is subject to controversy, and awaits exploration. The Russian-born mathematician and biologist Anatol Rapoport once remarked that general-system theory is not really a theory but instead "a program or a direction in the contemporary philosophy of science."

The concept of a system can be used to study patterns of interaction within and between units of foreign-policy decision making; by exploring such patterns, one can determine how foreign policies are formulated and how states or other units interact with or are related to each other, as opposed to how they interact with outside units. The members of a family, for example, interact with each other in ways that clearly differ from the ways in which they interact with other persons, such as colleagues in a place of employment or fellow members of a church. Although systems are definable in terms of units that exhibit certain patterns of interaction with each other, there also may be interaction between a system and its subsystems. A national political system, for example, may interact with subsystems such as interest groups, the media, or public opinion.

Systems and subsystems exist in a hierarchical setting. A department is a subsystem of a corporation, for example, just as a corporation is a subsystem of an industry. In international relations states are considered subsystems, or components, of the entire international system. In analyzing the international system, researchers often posit distinct political, economic, cultural, and social subsystems.

STRUCTURES, INSTITUTIONS, AND LEVELS OF ANALYSIS

Since the 1970s the study of international relations has been marked by a renewed debate about the relationship between structures and institutions in international systems. On one side of the controversy was a revival of the school of realism, known as neorealism. Neorealism represented an effort to inject greater precision, or conceptual rigour, into realist theory.

On the other side of the structures-institutions debate have been the neoliberal institutionalists, who contend that institutions matter beyond simply reflecting or codifying the power structure of the international system.

Although neorealist structuralists and neoliberal institutionalists generally agree that international cooperation is possible, neorealists are much more skeptical of its chances for long-term success.

CONSTRUCTIVISM

In the late 20th century the study of international relations was increasingly influenced by constructivism. Constructivists hold that all institutions, including the state, are socially constructed, in the sense that they reflect an "intersubjective consensus" of shared beliefs about political practice, acceptable social behaviour, and values. In much the same way, the individual members of the state or other unit continuously construct the reality about which policy decisions, including decisions about war and peace and conflict and cooperation, are made.

Part of the newer intellectual landscape in the study of international relations is formed by postmodernism and critical theory. According to postmodernism, the international structures posited in realist and other international relations theory are social constructions that reflect a worldview that serves the interests of elites. Critical theory was developed from the 1920s by the Frankfurt School of social and political philosophers, especially Jürgen Habermas and Herbert Marcuse (1898–1979). For critical theory the essential issue is how to emancipate human beings from social institutions and practices that oppress them. Although inspired by Marxism, critical theorists recognize forms of domination other than class domination, including those based on gender, race, religion, ethnicity, and nationalism. Because each of these forms has been in abundant evidence in the global landscape, critical theory was thought to provide important insights into the study of international relations at the start of the 21st century.

INTERNATIONAL POLITICAL ECONOMY

Nothing is more illustrative of the inherently interdisciplinary nature of international relations inquiry than the nexus between economic and political factors. Although politics and economics have been studied separately for analytic purposes and as academic disciplines, and although each has its own paradigms, theories, and methodologies, it has long been recognized that economic factors shape political decisions, just as political factors may have a decisive influence on economic choices. Writings on political economy proliferated from the rise of the modern state in the mid-17th century until the mid-19th century. Much of the literature emphasized mercantilism, the notion that economic activity is, or should be, subservient to the interests of the state. Influenced by the work of Adam Smith (1723–90), David Ricardo (1772–1823), Richard Cobden (1804–65), and John Stuart Mill (1806–73), political economists of this period developed a fundamentally different approach, known as economic liberalism, that held that a system of free trade supported by government policies of laissez-faire would lead to economic growth and expanded trade and make an important contribution to international peace. In the latter 19th century a third approach, based on the writings of Karl Marx, argued that an increasingly poor proletariat and an increasingly affluent bourgeoisie would eventually clash in a violent revolution resulting in the overthrow of the latter, the destruction of capitalism, and the emergence of communism.

Each of these sharply differing approaches has left its imprimatur on contemporary theories of international political economy. The earlier mercantilist approach influenced contemporary economic nationalism, which is characterized by several important assumptions: (1) states cannot remain powerful in an anarchic setting without a strong economy, (2) economic strength must be preserved by protecting key industries and jobs, (3) such protectionism may require tariffs and governmental subsidies, (4) low-priced imports may threaten domestic jobs and industry, (5) the state can and should remain sovereign in economic matters, and (6) membership in international economic organizations such as the WTO and agreements such as the North American Free Trade Agreement may have adverse consequences for national strength.

Contemporary economic liberalism shares with classical liberalism the contention that the only way a state can maximize economic growth is by allowing markets to operate free from government intervention. They maintain that tariffs—which have the effect of distorting the allocation of resources, production, and trade—restrict economic growth and should be abolished. Accordingly, they support the creation and expansion of regional and international free-trade organizations. Citing Ricardo's theory of comparative advantage and earlier ideas of Smith, they also argue that national specialization is essential to world prosperity because it entails that countries will produce only those goods and services they are best equipped to make, which thus maximizes overall efficiency and minimizes overall costs. More generally, liberals maintain that the basic units of the global economy are now so closely integrated that efforts on the part of states to restrict trade with other countries are bound to fail. Debate between economic nationalists and liberals centres on the extent to which the state, even if it can do so, should halt or reverse the forces leading to economic globalization.

The third basic contemporary approach to international political economy is rooted in Marxism, though the collapse of nearly all states with Marxist economies greatly undermined Marxist-inspired theories of international relations. Focusing on the relationship between wealthy states and impoverished ones, this approach, known as dependency theory, rejects the assumption that capitalism is the best means of economic development for impoverished states and instead argues that participation in international capitalism by poorer countries traps them in relationships of dependency and subordination to wealthier states.

CHAPTER FOUR

DOMESTIC POLITICS: PUBLIC OPINION

Public opinion is an aggregate of the individual views, attitudes, and beliefs about a particular topic, expressed by a significant proportion of a community. Some scholars treat the aggregate as a synthesis of the views of all or a certain segment of society; others regard it as a collection of many differing or opposing views. Writing in 1918, the American sociologist Charles Horton Cooley emphasized public opinion as a process of interaction and mutual influence rather than a state of broad agreement. The American political scientist V.O. Key, Jr., defined public opinion in 1961 as "opinions held by private persons which governments find it prudent to heed." Subsequent advances in statistical and demographic analysis led by the 1990s to an understanding of public opinion as the collective view of a defined population, such as a particular demographic or ethnic group. The influence of public opinion is not restricted to politics and elections. It is a powerful force in many other spheres, such as culture, fashion, literature and the arts, consumer spending, and marketing and public relations.

THEORETICAL AND PRACTICAL CONCEPTIONS

In his eponymous treatise on public opinion published in 1922, the American editorialist Walter Lippmann qualified his observation that democracies tend to make a mystery out of public opinion with the dec-

U.S. voters in 2012 brave the rain to participate in the presidential election.

laration that "there have been skilled organizers of opinion who understood the mystery well enough to create majorities on election day." Although the reality of public opinion is now almost universally accepted, there is much variation in the way it is defined, reflecting in large measure the different perspectives from which scholars have approached the subject. Contrasting understandings of public opinion have taken shape over the centuries, especially as new methods of measuring public opinion have been applied to politics, commerce, religion, and social activism.

Political scientists and some historians have tended to emphasize the role of public opinion in government and politics, paying particular

47

attention to its influence on the development of government policy. Indeed, some political scientists have regarded public opinion as equivalent to the national will. In such a limited sense, however, there can be only one public opinion on an issue at any given time.

Sociologists usually conceive of public opinion as a product of social interaction and communication. According to this view, there can be no public opinion on an issue unless members of the public communicate with each other. Even if their individual opinions are quite similar to begin with, their beliefs will not constitute a public opinion until they are conveyed to others in some form, whether through print media, radio, television, the Internet, or telephone or face-to-face conversation. Sociologists also point to the possibility of there being many different public opinions on a given issue at the same time. Although one body of opinion may dominate or reflect government policy, for example, this does not preclude the existence of other organized bodies of opinion on political topics. The sociological approach also recognizes the importance of public opinion in areas that have little or nothing to do with government.

Nearly all scholars of public opinion, regardless of the way they may define it, agree that, in order for a phenomenon to count as public opinion, at least four conditions must be satisfied: (1) there must be an issue, (2) there must be a significant number of individuals who express opinions on the issue, (3) there must be some kind of a consensus among at least some of these opinions, and (4) this consensus must directly or indirectly exert influence.

Those who aim to influence public opinion are more concerned with the practical problem of shaping the opinions of specified "publics," such as employees, stockholders, neighbourhood associations, or any other group whose actions may affect the fortunes of a client or stakeholder. Politicians and publicists, for example, seek ways to influence voting and purchasing decisions, respectively—hence their wish to determine any attitudes and opinions that may affect the desired behaviour.

It is often the case that opinions expressed in public differ from those expressed in private. Some views—even though widely shared—may not be expressed at all. Thus, in a totalitarian state, a great many people may be opposed to the government but may fear to express their attitudes even to their families and friends. In such cases, an antigovernment public opinion necessarily fails to develop.

THE FORMATION AND CHANGE OF PUBLIC OPINION

No matter how collective views coalesce into public opinion, the result can be self-perpetuating. The French political scientist Alexis de Tocqueville, for example, observed that once an opinion "has taken root among a democratic people and established itself in the minds of the bulk of the community, it afterwards persists by itself and is maintained without effort, because no one attacks it." In 1993 the German opinion researcher Elizabeth Noelle-Neumann characterized this phenomenon as a "spiral of silence," noting that people who perceive that they hold a minority view will be less inclined to express it in public.

COMPONENTS OF PUBLIC OPINION: ATTITUDES AND VALUES

The concepts of opinion, attitude, and value used in public opinion research were given an influential metaphorical characterization by the American-born political analyst Robert Worcester. Values, he suggested, are "the deep tides of public mood, slow to change, but powerful." Opinions, in contrast, are "the ripples on the surface of the public's consciousness—shallow and easily changed." Finally, attitudes are "the currents below the surface, deeper and stronger," representing a midrange between values and opinions. According to Worcester, the art of understanding public opinion rests not only on the measurement of people's views but also on understanding the motivations behind those views.

No matter how strongly they are held, attitudes are subject to change if the individual holding them learns of new facts or perspectives that challenge his or her earlier thinking. Some opinion researchers have contended that the standard technical concept of attitude is not useful for understanding public opinion, because it is insufficiently complex. Irving Crespi, for example, preferred to speak of "attitudinal systems," which he characterized as the combined development of four sets of phenomena: (1) values and interests, (2) knowledge and beliefs, (3) feelings, and (4) behavioral intentions (i.e., conscious inclinations to act in certain ways).

Perhaps the most important concept in public opinion research is that of values. Values are of considerable importance in determining whether people will form opinions on a particular topic; in general, they are more likely to do so when they perceive that their values require it. Values are adopted early in life, are not likely to change, and strengthen as people grow older. Values are relatively resistant to ordinary attempts at persuasion and to influence by the media, and they rarely shift as a result of positions or arguments expressed in a single debate. Yet they can be shaped—and in some cases completely changed—by prolonged exposure to conflicting values, by concerted thought and discussion, by the feeling that one is "out of step" with others whom one knows and respects, and by the development of significantly new evidence or circumstances.

FACTORS INFLUENCING PUBLIC OPINION

Public opinion is influenced by a variety of factors, including social environment, mass media, interest groups, and individual opinion leaders.

ENVIRONMENTAL FACTORS

Environmental factors play a critical part in the development of opinions and attitudes. Most pervasive is the influence of the social environment. People usually adjust their attitudes to conform to those that are most prevalent in the social groups to which they belong. Researchers have found, for example, that if a person in the United States who considers himself a liberal becomes surrounded in his home or at his place of work by people who profess conservatism, he is more likely to start voting for conservative candidates than is a liberal whose family and friends share his political views. Similarly, it was found during World War II that men in the U.S. military who transferred from one unit to another often adjusted their opinions to conform more closely to those of the unit to which they were transferred.

MASS MEDIA

The influence of mass media—including radio, television, and Internet-based social media, e-mail, and blogs—is significant, especially in affirming attitudes and opinions that are already established. The news media in particular focus the public's attention on certain personalities and issues, leading many people to form opinions about them. Government officials accordingly have noted that communications to them from the public tend to "follow the headlines."

51

The mass media can also reinforce latent attitudes and "activate" them, prompting people to take action, sometimes immediately. Just before an election, for example, voters who earlier had only a mild preference for one party or candidate may be inspired by media coverage not only to take the trouble to vote but perhaps also to contribute money or to help a party organization in some other way.

In some European countries the growth of broadcasting, especially television, affected the operation of the parliamentary system. Before television, national elections were seen largely as contests between a number of candidates or parties for parliamentary seats. As the electronic media grew more sophisticated technologically, elections increasingly assumed the appearance of a personal struggle between the leaders of the principal parties concerned. In the United States, presidential candidates have

Occupy Wall Street protesters (pictured in 2011) brought media attention to income inequality in the United States.

come to personify their parties.

In areas where the mass media are thinly spread, as in developing countries or in countries where the media are strictly controlled, word of mouth can sometimes perform the same functions as the press and broadcasting, though on a more limited scale. However social media have helped to magnify word of mouth particularly among younger citizens, with sometimes overwhelming results. For example, the pro-democracy protests that took place in several countries of the Middle East and North Africa in 2010-12 (the "Arab Spring") were frequently publicized and even coordinated through social media.

INTEREST GROUPS

Interest groups, nongovernmental organizations (NGOs), religious groups, and labour unions (trade unions) cultivate the formation and spread of public opinion on issues of concern to their constituencies. These groups may be concerned with political, economic, or ideological issues, and most work through the mass media as well as by word of mouth. Some of the larger or more affluent interest groups around the world make use of advertising and public relations. One increasingly popular tactic is the informal poll or straw vote. In this approach, groups ask their members and supporters to "vote"—usually by phone or via the Internet—in unsystematic "polls" of public opinion that are not carried out with proper sampling procedures. Multiple votes by supporters are often encouraged, and once the group releases its findings to credible media outlets, it claims legitimacy by citing the publication of its poll in a recognized newspaper or online news source.

OPINION LEADERS

Opinion leaders play a major role in defining popular issues and in influencing individual opinions regarding them. Political leaders in particular can turn a relatively unknown problem into a national issue if they decide to call attention to it in the media. One of the ways in which opinion leaders rally opinion and smooth out differences among those who are in basic agreement on a subject is by inventing symbols or coining slogans: in the words of U.S. Pres. Woodrow Wilson, the Allies in World War I were fighting "a war to end all wars," while aiming "to make the world safe for democracy"; post-World War II relations with the Soviet Union were summed up in the term "Cold War," first used by U.S. presidential adviser Bernard Baruch in 1947. Once enunciated, symbols and slogans are frequently kept alive and communicated to large audiences by the mass media and may become the cornerstone of public opinion on any given issue.

Opinion leadership is not confined to prominent figures in public life. An opinion leader can be any person to whom others look for guidance on a certain subject. Thus, within a given social group one person may be regarded as especially well-informed about local politics, another as knowledgeable about foreign affairs, and another as expert in real estate. These local opinion leaders are generally unknown outside their own circle of friends and acquaintances, but their cumulative influence in the formation of public opinion is substantial.

COMPLEX INFLUENCES

Because psychological makeup, personal circumstances, and external influences all play a role in the formation of each person's opinions, it is difficult to predict how public opinion on an issue will take shape. The same is true with regard to changes in public opinion. Some public opinions can be explained by specific events and circumstances, but in other cases the causes are more elusive. (Some opinions, however, are predictable: the public's opinions about other countries, for example, seem to depend largely on the state of relations between the governments involved. Hostile public attitudes do not cause poor relations—they are the result of them.)

People presumably change their own attitudes when they no longer seem to correspond with prevailing circumstances and, hence, fail to serve as guides to action. Similarly, a specific event, such as a natural disaster or a human tragedy, can heighten awareness of underlying problems or concerns and trigger changes in public opinion. Public opinion about the environment, for instance, has been influenced by single events such as the publication of Rachel Carson's *Silent Spring* in 1962; by the nuclear accident at Chernobyl, Ukraine, in 1986; by

AL GORE AND PUBLIC OPINION

Former Vice President Al Gore's presidential bid came to an unsuccessful end in 2000. Many attributed his loss to the personality war he had with George W. Bush, a candidate portrayed as fun, folksy, and charming. At the time, Gore was painted by conservatives as a wooden exaggerator who could not apply charm when needed. Though public opinion, hinging largely on personalities, cost Gore the presidential election, afterward he managed to change public opinion as he focused on his environmental work. Gore's public persona made a drastic change as he became a "rock star" of environmentalism, as well as an Oscar and Nobel Prize winner. Some in the media even affectionately dubbed him "the Goreacle."

Although the opinions of his political past still followed him, in 2015, the conservative Tea Party supported Gore's fight for solar power and other green energy sources. Tea Party organizer Debbie Dooley summed up her argument, "I want consumer choice, and clean air and clean water and solar is the best way to create a competitive choice." Public opinion on Gore's work evolved as his work came to be seen as environmentally important.

British Prime Minister Margaret Thatcher's 1988 address to the Royal Society on a number of environmental topics, including global warming; by the accidental spill from the oil tanker *Exxon Valdez* in 1989; by the Academy Award-winning documentary on climate change, *An Inconvenient Truth*, in 2006; and by the Arab Spring in 2010. It is nonetheless the case that whether a body of public opinion on a given issue is formed and sustained depends to a significant extent on the attention it receives in the mass media.

PUBLIC OPINION AND GOVERNMENT

By its very nature, the democratic process spurs citizens to form opinions on a number of issues. Voters are called upon to choose candidates in elections, to consider constitutional amendments, and to approve or reject municipal taxes and other legislative proposals. Almost any matter on which the executive or legislature has to decide may become a public issue if a significant number of people wish to make it one. The political attitudes of these persons are often stimulated or reinforced by outside agencies—a crusading newspaper, an interest group, or a government agency or official.

The English philosopher and economist Jeremy Bentham (1748–1832) saw the greatest difficulty of the legislator as being "in conciliating the public opinion, in correcting it when erroneous, and in giving it that bent which shall be most favourable to produce obedience to his mandates." At the same time, Bentham and some other thinkers believed that public opinion is a useful check on the authority of rulers. Bentham demanded that all official acts be publicized, so that an enlightened public opinion could pass judgment on them, as would a tribunal: "To the pernicious exercise of the power of government it is the only check."

In the early years of modern democracy, some scholars acknowledged the power of public opinion but warned that it could be a dangerous force. Tocqueville was concerned that a government of the masses would become a "tyranny of the majority." But, whether public opinion is regarded as a constructive or a baneful force in a democracy, there are few politicians who are prepared to suggest in public that government should ignore it.

Political scientists have been less concerned with what part public opinion should play in a democratic polity and have given more attention to establishing what part it does play in actuality. From the examination of numerous histories of policy formation, it is clear that no sweeping generalization can be made that will hold in all cases. The role of public opinion varies from issue to issue, just as public opinion asserts itself differently from one democracy to another. Perhaps the safest generalization that can be made is that public opinion does not influence the details of most government policies but it does set limits within which policy makers must operate. That is, public officials will usually seek to satisfy a widespread demand—or at least take it into account in their deliberations—and they will usually try to avoid decisions that they believe will be widely unpopular.

Yet efforts by political leaders to accommodate government policies to public opinion are not always perceived as legitimate; indeed, journalists and political commentators have often characterized them as pandering to public opinion to curry favour with their constituents or as being driven by the latest poll results. Such charges were questioned, however, by public opinion scholars Lawrence R. Jacobs and Robert Y. Shapiro, who argued in *Politicians Don't Pander: Political Manipulation and the Loss of Democratic Responsiveness* (2000) that politicians do not actually do this. They found instead that by the early 1970s the accusation of pandering was being used deliberately by prominent journalists, politicians, and other elites as a means of lessening the influence of public opinion on government policy. This practice, they theorized, might have resulted from long-standing suspicion or hostility among elites

POLITICAL POLLS

Polls conducted on the eve of voting day have been successful in forecasting election results in nearly every case in which they have been used for this purpose. Some notable failures occurred in the United States in 1948 (when nearly all polls forecast a Republican victory and the Democrats won by a narrow margin) and in Great Britain in 1970 (when all but one of the major polls incorrectly predicted a Labour Party victory) and again in 1992 (when all polls incorrectly predicted a hung parliament). Professional opinion researchers point out that predicting elections is always uncertain, because of the possibility of last-minute shifts of opinion and unexpected turnouts on voting day; nevertheless, their record has been good over the years in nearly every country.

Although popular attention has been focused on polls taken before major elections, most polling is devoted to other subjects, and university-based opinion researchers usually do not make election forecasts at all. Support for opinion studies comes largely from public agencies, foundations, and commercial firms, which are interested in questions such as how well people's health, educational, and other needs are being satisfied, how problems such as racial prejudice and drug addiction should be addressed, and how well a given industry is meeting public demands.

toward popular participation in government and politics. In keeping with their findings, Jacobs and Shapiro postulated the eventual disappearance from public discourse of the stigmatizing term *pandering* and its replacement by the more neutral term *political responsiveness*.

Harry Truman holds the *Chicago Daily Tribune*, which erroneously reported he was beaten for the presidency.

Although they rejected the charge of pandering, Jacobs and Shapiro also asserted that most politicians tend to respond to public opinion in cynical ways; most of them, for example, use public opinion research not to establish their policies but only to identify slogans and symbols that will make predetermined policies more appealing to their constituents. According to Jacobs and Shapiro, most public opinion research is used to manipulate the public rather than to act on its wishes.

Public opinion exerts a more powerful influence in politics through its "latent" aspects. As discussed by V.O. Key, Jr., latent public opinion is, in effect, a probable future reaction by the public to a current decision or action by a public official or a government. Politicians who ignore the possible consequences of latent public opinion risk setback or defeat in future elections. Government leaders who take latent public opinion into account, on the other hand, may be willing to undertake an unpopular action that has a negative effect on public opinion in the near term, provided that the action is also likely to have a significant positive effect at a later and more important time.

Public opinion seems to be much more effective in influencing policy making at the local level than at the state or national levels. One reason for this is that issues of concern to local governments—such as the condition of roads, schools, and hospitals—are less complex than those dealt with by governments at higher levels; another is that at the local level there are fewer institutional or bureaucratic barriers between policy makers and voters. Representative government itself, however, tends to limit the power of public opinion to influence specific government decisions, since ordinarily the only choice the public is given is that of approving or disapproving the election of a given official.

PUBLIC OPINION POLLING

Public opinion polling can provide a fairly exact analysis of the distribution of opinions on almost any issue within a given population. Assuming that the proper questions are asked, polling can reveal something about the intensity with which opinions are held, the reasons for these opinions, and the probability that the issues have been discussed with others. Polling can occasionally reveal whether the people holding an opinion can be thought of as constituting a cohesive group. However, survey findings do not provide much information about the opinion leaders who may have played an important part in developing the opinion (although this information may be obtained through subgroup analysis, provided that the original sample is large enough to ensure that reports of opinion leaders are statistically reliable to a reasonable degree).

Polls are good tools for measuring "what" or "how much." Finding out "how" or "why," however, is the principal function of qualitative research—including especially the use of focus groups—which involves observing interactions between a limited number of people rather than posing a series of questions to an individual in an in-depth interview. However, polls cannot identify the likely future actions of the public in general, nor can they predict the future behaviour of individuals. They are also inappropriate as tools for exploring concepts unfamiliar to respondents. One of the best predictors of how people will vote is, simply, the vote that they cast in the last election. This is especially true if they automatically vote for the same political party.

CHAPTER FIVE

DOMESTIC POLITICS: ELECTIONS

Elections make a fundamental contribution to democratic governance. Because direct democracy—a form of government in which political decisions are made directly by the entire body of qualified citizens—is impractical in most modern societies, democratic government must be conducted through representatives. Elections enable voters to select leaders and to hold them accountable for their performance in office. Elections also reinforce the stability and legitimacy of the political community. They link citizens to each other and thereby confirm the viability of the polity. As a result, elections help to facilitate social and political integration. Elections also serve a self-actualizing purpose by confirming the worth and dignity of individual citizens as human beings.

TYPES OF ELECTIONS

In elections of officeholders, the electorates have only a limited power to determine government policies. Most elections do not directly establish public policy but instead confer on a small group of officials the authority to make policy (through laws and other devices) on behalf of the electorate as a whole.

Recall elections are an attempt to minimize the influence of political parties on representatives. Widely adopted in the United States, the recall is designed to ensure that an elected official will act in the interests of his constituency rather than in the interests of his political party or according to his own conscience. The actual instrument of recall is usually a letter of resignation signed by the elected representative before assuming office. During the term of office, the letter can be evoked by a quorum of constituents if the representative's performance fails to meet their expectations.

The referendum and initiative are elections in which the preferences of the community are assessed on a particular issue; whereas the former are instigated by those in government, the latter are initiated by groups of electors. Referenda often are used for bond issues to raise and spend public money, though occasionally they are used to decide certain social

In Fort Lauderdale, Fla., a ballot is scrutinized during a recount of the U.S. presidential election, November 2000.

or moral issues—such as restrictions on abortion or divorce—on which the elected bodies are deemed to possess no special competence.

Plebiscites are elections held to decide two paramount types of political issues: government legitimacy and the nationality of territories contested between governments. In the former case, the incumbent government, seeking a popular mandate as a basis for legitimacy, employs a plebiscite to establish its right to speak for the nation. In the latter case, plebiscites have decided the nationality of territories such as after World

War I when the League of Nations proposed 11 plebiscites. This use of plebiscites, however, is relatively rare, because it requires the prior agreement of the governments involved.

SYSTEMS OF VOTE COUNTING

Individual votes are translated into collective decisions by a wide variety of rules of counting that voters and leaders have accepted as legitimate prior to the election. These rules may in principle call for plurality voting, which requires only that the winner have the greatest number of votes; absolute majority voting, which requires that the winner receive more than half the total number of votes; extraordinary majority voting, which requires some higher proportion for the winner (e.g., a two-thirds majority); proportional voting, which requires that a political party receive some threshold to receive representation; or unanimity.

LEGISLATIVE ELECTIONS

A wide variety of electoral systems exist for apportioning legislative seats. In practice, legislative electoral systems can be classified into three broad categories: plurality and majority systems, collectively known as majoritarian systems (in which the party or candidate winning a plurality or majority of votes in a constituency is awarded the contested seat); proportional systems (in which the distribution of seats is broadly proportional to the distribution of the vote among competing political parties); and hybrid, or semiproportional, systems. The electoral system is an important variable in explaining public policy decisions, because it determines the number of political parties able to receive representation and thereby participate in government.

EXECUTIVE ELECTIONS

In the parliamentary system, the head of government or head of State is selected by the legislature. For example, in Germany the president is selected by both the upper and the lower chamber of the legislature. By contrast, in Ireland the president is elected by a plurality vote of the public.

In presidential systems and mixed (semipresidential) systems, the head of state is elected independently of the legislature. Several methods of electing presidents have been adopted. In the simplest method, the plurality system, which is used in Mexico and the Philippines, the candidate with the most votes wins election. In France the president is required to win a majority. Both the plurality and the majority-decision rules are employed in the election of U.S. presidents, who are elected only indirectly by the public. The composition of the electoral college, which actually selects the president, is determined by a plurality vote taken within each state. Although voters choose between the various presidential candidates, they are in effect choosing the electors who will elect the president by means of a majority vote in the electoral college. With the exception of Maine and Nebraska, all of a state's electoral votes (which are equal in number to its seats in Congress) are awarded to the presidential candidate who gains a plurality of the vote in the state election. It is thus possible for a president to be elected with a minority of the popular vote.

CONSTITUENCIES: DISTRICTING AND APPORTIONMENT

The drawing up of constituencies—the subdivisions of the total electorate that send representatives to the local or central assembly—is inex-

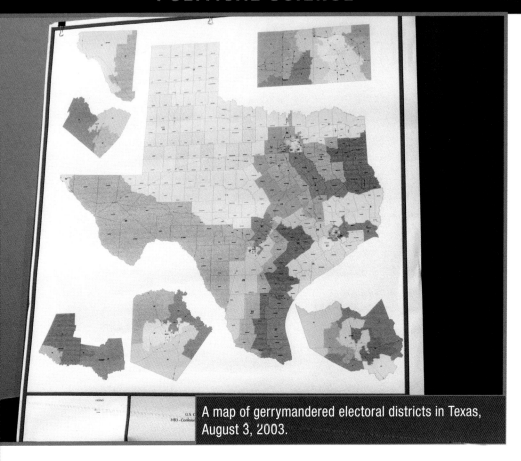

A map of gerrymandered electoral districts in Texas, August 3, 2003.

tricably linked with questions about the nature of representation and methods of voting. The problem of electoral representation hinges on the question of what is to be represented. As geographic areas, constituencies often contain within their boundaries diverse, and sometimes incompatible, social, economic, religious, or ethnic interests, all of which seek to be represented.

The solution to this problem has been largely historically determined. Where the interests of electors have not been totally incompatible, and where ethnic, religious, social, and economic differences have been relatively free of passionate conflict, geographic areas (electoral districts) have usually been considered the constituency, and the method of counting has been some system of majority or plurality voting. In contrast, where the electorate is composed of several minorities, none of which can hope to obtain a majority, or perhaps not even a plurality sufficiently large to obtain representation, the geographic district can be regarded only as an administrative unit for counting votes.

The drawing up, or delimitation, of electoral districts is linked with differing conceptions of representation, and conceptions of representation in turn are linked with alternative methods of vote counting. Problems of apportionment, in contrast to problems of districting, stem from efforts to reconcile the territorial and population bases of representation. During the 19th and much of the 20th century, failure to reapportion the number of seats in representative bodies to take account of population changes resulting from increasing urbanization generally benefitted rural electoral districts. More recently, the migration of people from cities to the suburbs has led to possible underrepresentation of suburban populations as against urban ones.

Apportionment is often a complex problem. In particular, it is often unclear how best to define the population among which a specified number of legislative seats are to be apportioned. Constitutional or electoral malapportionment must not be confused with gerrymandering—a form of arbitrary districting used to benefit the party that at a given time controls the apportionment process. Gerrymandering takes its name from the governor of Massachusetts Elbridge Gerry (1744–1814), who recognized the possibility of influencing electoral outcomes by manipulating the boundaries of electoral districts (critics charged that one of the districts he designed resembled a salamander). Gerrymandering involves concentrating large percentages of the opposite party's votes into a few districts and drawing the boundaries of the other districts in such a way that the gerrymandering party wins them all, even though the majority, or, in multiparty elections, the plurality, is relatively small.

VOTING PRACTICES

There is a direct relationship between the size of an electorate and the formalization and standardization of its voting practices. In very small voting groups, in which political encounters are face-to-face and the members are bound together by ties of friendship or common experience, political discussion is mostly informal and may not even require formal voting, because the "sense of the meeting" emerges from the group's deliberations. An issue is discussed until a solution emerges to which all participants can agree or, at least, from which any one participant will not dissent.

By contrast, in modern mass electorates, in which millions of individual votes are aggregated into a collective choice, formalization and standardization of voting practices and vote counting are required to ensure that the outcome is valid, reliable, and legitimate. Validity means that the collective choice in fact expresses the will of the electorate; reliability refers to each vote's being accurately recorded and effectively counted; and legitimacy means that the criteria of validity and reliability have been met, so that the result of the voting is acceptable and provides authoritative guidelines in subsequent political conduct. In some countries that hold elections, observers have reported irregularities in the counting of votes and have questioned the legitimacy of the results. For example, one study of the U.S. presidential election of 2000 between Al Gore and G.W. Bush found that millions of votes were uncounted as a result of outdated election equipment, registration errors, and other problems, which led some critics to argue that the outcome was illegitimate.

Routinized and standardized electoral practices in mass electorates were developed beginning in the mid-19th century. Their development was as much a corollary of the growth of rapid communication through telephone and telegraph as of the growth of the electorate and rational insistence on making electoral processes fair and equitable. Nevertheless, electoral practices around the world differ a great deal, depending not just on formal institutional arrangements but even more on a country's political culture.

People line up to vote in the U.S. presidential election in 2012.

SECRET VOTING

Once suffrage rights had been extended to masses of voters who, in theory, were assumed to be equal, open voting was no longer tolerable, precisely because it could and often did involve undue influence, ranging from hidden persuasion and bribery to intimidation, coercion, and punishment. Equality, at least in voting, was not something given but something that had to be engineered; the secrecy of the vote was a first and necessary administrative step toward the one person, one vote principle. Equality in voting was possible only if each vote was formally independent of every other vote, and this suggested the need for strict secrecy.

Secret voting dramatically reduces the possibility of undue influence on the voter. Without it, influence can range from the outright purchase of votes to social chastisement or economic sanctions. Although laws exist in most countries to prohibit and punish the purchase or sale of votes, the introduction of secret voting has not wholly eliminated bribery.

BALLOTING

The ballot makes secret voting possible. Its initial use seems to have been as a means to reduce irregularities and deception in elections. However, this objective could be achieved only if the ballot was not supplied by the voter himself, as was the case in much early voting by secret ballot, or by political parties, as is still the case in some countries. Ballot procedures differ widely, ranging from marking the names of preferred candidates to crossing out those not preferred or writing in the names of persons who are not formal candidates. Some ballots require the selection of one or more candidates or parties or both, and others require the preferential ordering of a number of candidates.

The introduction of voting machines and computer technology has not substantially changed the balloting process, though it generally has made it faster and more economical. Voting machines are not without problems, in that they may marginally depress the level of voting owing to improper use, a problem that can be overcome through improved machines and voter education.

COMPULSORY VOTING

In some countries, notably Australia and Belgium, electoral participation is legally required, and nonvoters can face fines. The concept of compulsory voting reflects a strain in democratic theory in which voting is considered not merely a right but a duty. Its purpose is to ensure the electoral equality of all social groups. However, whether created through laws or through social pressure, it is doubtful that high voter turnout is a good indication of an electorate's capability for intelligent social choice. On the other hand, high rates of abstention or differential rates of abstention by different social classes are not necessarily signs of satisfaction with governmental processes and policies and in fact may indicate the contrary.

ELECTORAL ABUSES

Corrupt electoral practices are not limited to bribery or voter intimidation. They include disseminating scurrilous rumours and false campaign propaganda, tampering with election machinery by stuffing ballot boxes with fraudulent returns, counting or reporting the vote dishonestly, and disregarding electoral outcomes by incumbent officeholders (e.g., by mobilizing the military to thwart an election loss). The existence of these practices depends more on a population's adherence to political civility and the democratic ethos than on legal prohibitions and sanctions. The integrity of the electoral process can be maintained by a variety of devices and practices, including a permanent and up-to-date register of voters and procedures designed to make the registration process as simple as possible.

PARTICIPATION IN ELECTIONS

Electoral participation rates depend on many factors, including the type of electoral system, the social groupings to which voters belong, the voters' personalities and beliefs, their places of residence, and a host of other idiosyncratic factors.

The level and type of election have a great impact on the rate of electoral participation. Electoral turnout is greater in national than in state or provincial elections, and greater in the latter than in local elections.

71

VOTER ID LAWS

A voter identification law is any U.S. state law by which would-be voters are required or requested to present proof of their identities before casting a ballot. Proponents of voter ID laws argue that they are necessary to prevent in-person voter fraud and that they would increase public confidence in the integrity of the electoral system. Opponents point out that in-person voter fraud is virtually nonexistent and argue that the real purpose of such laws is to suppress voting among Democratic-leaning groups such as African Americans, the poor, and the young, a greater proportion of whom do not possess the relevant forms of identification.

If local elections are held concurrently with provincial or national elections, generally a higher voter turnout is achieved than for nonconcurrent elections. Whether an election is partisan or nonpartisan also affects turnout, as fewer people participate in nonpartisan elections.

Technicalities in the electoral law may disenfranchise many potential voters. For example, people who change their legal residence may temporarily lose their vote because of residence requirements for voters in their new electoral district. Complicated voter-registration procedures, combined with a high level of geographic mobility, significantly reduce the size of the active electorate in the United States. In the early 21st century many U.S. states also implemented voter ID laws, which required would-be voters to present some form of identification at polling places as a condition of voting; these measures too had the effect of reducing the number of eligible or active voters. In contrast, in many other countries the size of the electorate is maximized by government-initiated registration immediately prior to an election. Voter registration in the United States is largely left to the initiative of individuals and political parties. In the early 19th century, slaves were denied the right to vote, as were newly naturalized nonwhite citizens. Even freed slaves were denied this right, though mainly in slave-owning southern states. Even after African Americans were granted suffrage, southern laws subjected them to arbitrary examinations, their votes thrown out, and voters were sometimes beaten or murdered. Voter registration requirements continue to be hotly debated, as some say they negatively affect minorities and the poor.

Relatively low levels of electoral participation are associated with low levels of education, occupational status, and income. Those groups in society that have been most recently enfranchised also tend to vote at lower rates. For a significant period of time in the 20th century, women voted less frequently than men, though the difference had been erased by the end of the century in most countries. The rates of participation of racial minorities are generally lower than those of majority groups, and members of the working class vote less frequently than members of the middle class. In many countries, participation by young people is significantly lower than that of older people.

Voter participation varies from country to country. For example, approximately half of the voting-age population participates in presidential elections in the United States. In contrast, many European countries have participation rates exceeding 80 percent. Even within Europe, however, participation varies significantly. For example, post-World War II Italy has averaged around 90 percent, whereas less than 40 percent of the electorate participates in elections in Switzerland. Research has suggested a long-term decline in turnout at national elections in western democracies since the 1970s; it seems most likely that this is a consequence of partisan dealignment (i.e., a weakening of partisan identification), the erosion of social cleavages based on class and religion, and increasing voter discontent.

INFLUENCES ON VOTING BEHAVIOUR

The electoral choices of voters are influenced by a range of factors, especially social-group identity, which helps to forge enduring partisan identification. In addition, voters are to a greater or lesser extent susceptible to the influence of more short-term and contingent factors such as campaign events, issues, and candidate appeals. In particular, the perceived governing competence of candidates and political parties often weighs heavily on voters' choices.

Research suggests that, through partisan dealignment, the proportion of voters in Western democracies who retain their long-term partisan identities has been reduced. In conjunction with the declining impact of social-group influences, voter choice is now more heavily affected by short-term factors relevant to specific election campaigns. This shift from long-term predisposition to short-term evaluation has been facilitated in part by the phenomenon of "cognitive mobilization," a supposed enhancement of the political independence and intelligence of voters who are both better educated and better informed than earlier generations. Nevertheless, many independents and nonvoters are poorly informed politically and relatively uninterested and uninvolved in politics. Whether cognitively mobilized or not, however, independent voters are often a decisive factor in elections. If elections are to be competitive, and if control of the government is to alternate between parties or coalitions of parties, then some voters must switch party support from election to election. New voters and independent voters, therefore, provide a vital source of change in democratic politics.

CHAPTER SIX

DOMESTIC POLITICS: GOVERNMENT

G overnment is the political system by which a country or community is administered and regulated. Most of the key words commonly used to describe governments—words such as *monarchy, oligarchy,* and *democracy*—are of Greek or Roman origin. They have been current for more than 2,000 years and have not yet exhausted their usefulness. This suggests that humankind has not altered very much since they were coined; however, such verbal and psychological uniformity must not be allowed to hide the enormous changes in society and politics that have occurred. Understanding any of these political terms, however, requires an investigation of the circumstances that have predisposed societies to adopt or reject the system of government in question.

AGRICULTURAL SOCIETY

So long as humans were few, there was hardly any government. The division of function between ruler and ruled occurred only, if at all, within the family. The largest social groups, whether tribes or villages, were little more than loose associations of families, in which every elder or family head had an equal voice. Chieftains, if any, had strictly limited powers; some tribes did without chieftains altogether.

The rise of agriculture began to change that state of affairs. In the land of Sumer (in what is now Iraq) the invention of irrigation necessitated grander arrangements. Control of the flow of water down the Tigris and Euphrates rivers had to be coordinated by a central authority, so that fields could be watered downstream as well as farther up. The heads of the first cities, which were little more than enlarged villages, only gradually assumed the special attributes of monarchy—the rule of one—and the village council only gradually undertook a division of labour, so that some specialized as priests and others as warriors, farmers, or tax gatherers. As organization grew more complex, so did religion: an elaborate system of worship seemed necessary to propitiate the gods who, it was hoped, would protect the city from attack, from natural disaster, and from any questioning of the political arrangements deemed necessary by the ruler group. Inevitably, the young cities of Sumer quarrelled over the distribution of the rivers' water, and their wealth excited the greed of nomads outside the still comparatively small area of civilization. War announced its arrival, and military leadership became at least as important an element of kingship as divine sanction. The wars of Sumer also laid bare another imperative of monarchy—the drive for empire, arising from the need to defend and the need to find new means to pay for troops and weapons.

THE SPREAD OF CIVILIZATION

The history of Old World monarchy, and indeed of civilization, was to consist largely of variations on the patterns mentioned above for four or five millennia. The effort to secure a measure of peace and prosperity required the assertion of authority over vast distances, the raising of large armies, and the gathering of taxes to pay for them. Those requirements in turn fostered literacy and numeracy and the emergence of what later came to be called bureaucracy—government by officials. Bureaucratic imperialism emerged again and again and spread with civilization. Barbarian challenge occasionally laid it low but never for very long. When one city or people rose to hegemony over its neighbours, it simply incorporated their bureaucracy into its own. Sumer and Babylon were conquered by Assyria; Assyria was overthrown by the Medes of Persia, in alliance with a resurgent Babylon and nomadic Scythians; the empire of

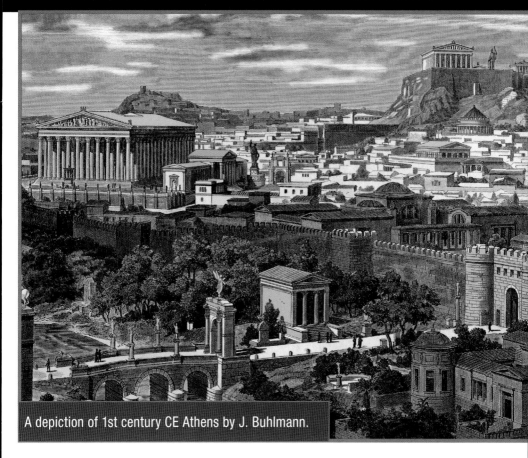

A depiction of 1st century CE Athens by J. Buhlmann.

the Persians was overthrown by Alexander the Great (356–323 BCE) of Macedonia; the Macedonian successor states were conquered by Rome, which was in due course supplanted in the Middle East and North Africa by the Islamic Caliphate of Baghdad. Conquerors came and went, but life for their subjects, whether peasants or townspeople, was not much altered by anything they did, as long as the battles happened elsewhere.

Nevertheless, from time to time experiments were made, for no monarchy had the resources to rule all its subjects directly. So long as they paid tribute punctually, local rulers and local communities were perforce left to govern themselves.

THE CITY-STATES OF GREECE

The city-state (*polis* in Greek, from which the term *politics* derives) was the great political invention of classical antiquity. The city-state was made possible by Mediterranean geography, which is such that every little fishing village had to be able to defend itself against attack from land or sea. Each city-state was, on the one hand, an economic, cultural, and religious organization; on the other hand, each was a self-governing community capable, in theory, of maintaining absolute independence by enlisting all its adult male inhabitants as soldiers. Although it was a fact of the Greek world that geography deterred the rise of an empire to federate and control all the cities, a few nevertheless rose to imperial greatness. Athens was one of these. During the period of its prime Athens was free to make what experiments it liked in the realm of government, and to that period are owed not just the first example of successful democracy in world history but also the first investigations in political thought.

ROME AND THE REPUBLIC

But, as it turned out, the city-state had barely begun to display its full political potential. To the west, two non-Greek cities, Carthage and Rome, began to struggle for mastery, and, after the defeat of the Carthaginian general Hannibal at Zama (202 BCE), Rome emerged as the strongest state in the Mediterranean.

The Greek historian Polybius suggested that Rome's constitution was such a success because it was a judicious blend of monarchy, aristocracy, and democracy. The Romans, a conservative, practical people, showed what they thought of such abstractions by speaking only of an unanalyzed "public thing"—*res publica*—and thus gave a new word, *republic*, to politics. With this focus the patriotism of the city-state reached its greatest intensity.

Wars, always supposedly in self-defense, had gradually extended Rome's power over Italy, and led to conquests and widening of Rome's lands. But the strains of empire building led to an end to the republic and the beginning of the monarchy of Augustus. The bedrock of the emperor Augustus's power was his command of the legions with which he had defeated all his rivals, but he was a much better politician than he was a general. He reduced the military establishment, laboured to turn the revolutionary faction that had supported his bid for power into a respectable new ruling class, and proclaimed the restoration of the republic in 27 BCE. However Augustus never went so far as to restore genuinely free elections or the organs of popular government. Like earlier monarchs elsewhere, he called in the aid of religion to legitimize his monarchy.

Four centuries later, the age of the city-state was at last drawing to a close. The emperor Caracalla extended Roman citizenship to all subjects of the empire, so that he could tax them more heavily. The demands of the imperial administration began to bankrupt the cities, new barbarian attacks threw the empire onto the defensive, and in 410 CE the city of Rome itself was captured and sacked by the Visigoths. About 65 years later the last Roman emperor in the West was deposed, and thenceforward the caesars reigned only in Constantinople and the East.

THE MIDDLE AGES

Seen against the background of the millennia, the fall of the Roman Empire was so commonplace an event that it is almost surprising that so much ink has been spilled in the attempt to explain it. What really needs explaining is the fact that the Western Empire was never restored.

DISSOLUTION AND INSTABILITY

Imperial thrones were never vacant for long. In China, after every time of troubles, a new dynasty received "the mandate of heaven," and a new emperor, or "son of heaven," rebuilt order. Similar patterns mark the history of India and Japan. When Justinian I, the greatest of the Eastern Roman (Byzantine) emperors, reconquered large portions of the West in the 6th century his soldiers made things worse rather than better. In 800 Charlemagne, king of the Franks, was actually crowned emperor of the Romans by the pope. In later centuries the Hohenstaufen and Habsburg dynasties tried to restore the empire, and as late as the 19th century so did Napoleon I. None of those attempts succeeded. Britain fell away from the empire in the 5th century; the little kingdoms of the Angles and Saxons were just coming together as one kingdom, England, when the Viking invasions began. In the 7th century the Arabs conquered North Africa; in the 8th they took Spain and invaded Gaul. Lombards, Avars, Slavs, Bulgars, and Magyars poured into Europe from the east. Not until German king Otto I's victory over the Magyars at Lechfeld in 955 did those incursions cease, and not until the late 11th century was Latin Christendom more or less secure within its borders, and by then it had been without an effective emperor for more than 600 years.

FEUDALISM

Various institutions had emerged to fill the gap. The Christian church, against enormous odds, had kept the light of religion and learning alive and spread what was left of Roman civilization into Ireland, England, central Europe, and Scandinavia. It also provided a reservoir of literacy against the day when professional government should again be possible. The kings of the barbarians, of whom Charlemagne was the greatest, had provided military leadership and tried to acquire some of the prestige and governmental machinery of the Roman emperors. But the troublous times, during which trade and urban life were minimal, meant that effective power lay with those who controlled the land and its products: a military aristocracy of great estates and fiefs (Latin *feodum*, hence "feudal system"). The aristocrats called themselves *nobiles* in the Roman fashion and appropriated various late imperial titles, such as *comes* (count) and *dux* (duke). But those titles were mere decoration. The new kings, lacking the machinery for imperial taxation, could not pay for standing armies. Hired knights waged war. Europe fell under the rule of these armoured knights, and the course of the next few hundred years gives reason to think that the democrats of Greece were right to distrust the very idea of oligarchy, for the keynote of noble rule seemed to be almost incessant warfare.

THE RISE OF LAW AND THE NATION-STATE

Yet even at their height the military aristocrats never had it all their own way. Medieval Europe was a constantly shifting kaleidoscope of political arrangements operating on the principle that because everybody's claim to power and property was fragile and inconsistent with everybody else's, a certain degree of mutual forbearance was necessary. However, the evolving Europe of privileged orders was also the Europe of rising monarchies. Kings clawed power to themselves; by 1500 most of them presided over bureaucracies (initially staffed by clerics) that would have impressed any Roman emperor. But universal empire was still impossible. The foundations of the new monarchies were purely territorial. Attempts at forced authority caused several wars, and Spanish kings tried to force uniformity by way of the Catholic religion. That uniformity paved the way for the most characteristic governmental form of the modern world, the nation-state.

Marie Antoinette being led to the guillotine on October 16, 1793.

THE RISE AND FALL OF ABSOLUTE MONARCHY

The development of the nation-state was not easy, for the monarchs or anyone else. Monarchs did all they could to resist the rise of representative institutions—except in England, where Henry VIII and the other Tudor monarchs worked with Parliament to make laws and where the folly of the Stuart kings ultimately ensured Parliament's supremacy. On the whole, however, the monarchs of Europe—especially in France, Spain, Prussia, and Austria—had great success at ruling autocratically. Their style of rule, known as absolute monarchy or absolutism, was a system in which the monarch was supposed to be supreme, in both lawmaking and policy making.

Absolutism lasted into the 18th century. Well before that time, though, three great occurrences—the Renaissance, the Reformation, and the discovery of the Americas—had transformed Europe. The truest symbol of the Renaissance's importance is the printing press. This invention enormously increased the resources of government. Laws, for instance, could be circulated far more widely and more accurately than ever before. More important still was the fact that the printing press increased the size of the educated and literate classes. Renaissance civilization thus became something unprecedented: it acquired deeper foundations than any of its predecessors or contemporaries on any continent by calling into play the intelligence of more individuals than ever before. But the catch (from a ruler's point of view) was that this development also brought public opinion into being for the first time.

The Reformation was the eldest child of the press. It, too, had diffuse and innumerable consequences, the most important of which was the destruction of the Roman Catholic Church's effective claim to universality. The consequence was the secularization of politics and administration and the introduction of some measure of religious toleration. Gradually the way became clear for rational, utilitarian considerations to shape government.

The discovery of the Americas opened a new epoch in world history. Portuguese and Spanish explorations gave far-flung overseas empires to both countries—and as many difficulties as benefits. Other countries—France, England, the Netherlands, Sweden, and Denmark—thought it both undesirable and unsafe not to seek such empire themselves, and the Iberian monarchies were thus involved in a perpetual struggle to defend their acquisitions. However, this stretched the kingdoms' revenues and inadequacies of the monarchical system, notably their ability to effectively rule or quell revolts, had been cruelly exposed.

REPRESENTATION AND CONSTITUTIONAL MONARCHY

Meanwhile, the republican tradition had never quite died out. The Dutch emerged from a long struggle against Spain clinging triumphantly to their new religion and their ancient constitution, a somewhat ramshackle federation known as the United Provinces. Switzerland was another medieval confederation. Venice and Genoa were rigidly oligarchical republics.

In England the rise of Parliament introduced a republican, if not a democratic, element into the workings of one of Europe's oldest kingdoms. The tradition of representative estates was first exploited by the Renaissance monarchy of Henry VIII and his children, the Tudors, and then unsuccessfully challenged by their successors, the Stuarts. After a series of upheavals, William III, a Dutchman, conceded full power of the purse to the House of Commons. A radically new age had dawned. Henceforth the country was to be ruled by a partnership between king and Parliament later known as constitutional monarchy.

THE AMERICAN AND FRENCH REVOLUTIONS

The limited British monarchy found it little easier to govern a seaborne empire than did the kings of France and Spain. If Britain's North American colonies were to grow in population and riches—so as to become sources of strength to the empire, not military and financial liabilities—they had to be given a substantial measure of religious, economic, and political autonomy. However, that gift could not be revoked. Once a chain of more or less self-governing communities had been created, it could not be undone. Thus, when the British government attempted to impose tighter rule from London, the Anglo-Americans fought with determination and good luck against their former overlord, King George III, and in 1776 their leaders determined to be rid of him and the British Parliament forever. The principles on which they meant to found a new commonwealth were expounded in their Declaration of Independence.

The American example might have had little effect on Europe but for the French Revolution of 1789. The French had helped the Americans defeat the British, but the effort had been too much in the end for the monarchy's finances. To avert state bankruptcy the Estates-General were summoned for the first time in 175 years, and soon the whole government had been turned upside down. The French repudiated the divine right of kings, the ascendancy of the nobility, the privileges of the Roman Catholic Church, and the regional structure of old France. Finally, they set up a republic and executed the king and queen.

The kings had created the French state; the revolution made it stronger than ever. The kings had united their subjects in the quest for glory; now the nation made the quest its own. In the name of rationality, liberty, and equality (fraternity was not a foremost concern), France again went to war. Yet, on the whole, the work of the French Revolution survived.

However many changes of regime France endured (seven between 1814 and 1870), its institutions had been thoroughly democratized.

NATIONALISM AND IMPERIALISM

The kingdom of Prussia and the empires of Austria and Russia readily learned from the French Revolution that it was necessary to rationalize government. They had been struggling along that path even before 1789. The great dynasts, and the military aristocracies that supported them, had no intention of admitting their obsolescence, though they were forced to make limited concessions between 1789 and World War I.

Nationalism intensified the competitiveness that had always been a part of the European state system. Peoples, it emerged, could be as touchy about their prestige as monarchs. But for one hundred years there was no general war in Europe, leaving the powers free to pursue interests in other parts of the world. Asia and Africa thus came to feel the full impact of European expansion, as the Americas had felt it before. Only the Japanese proved to have the skill to adapt successfully to the new ways—taking what suited them and rejecting the rest. The Netherlands, Spain, and Portugal clung to what they had, though the last two suffered great imperial losses as Mexico, Brazil, and other Latin American colonies shook off imperial rule. It seemed that before long the whole world would be ruled by half a dozen powers.

It did not remain so for long. The problem of governmental legitimacy in central, eastern, and southern Europe was too explosive. The obstinate conservatism of the dynasts proved fatal to more than monarchy. Authority itself, corrupted by power and at the same time gnawingly aware of its own fragility, gambled on militarist adventures. The upshot was World War I and the revolutions that resulted from it, especially those in Russia in March and November 1917, which overthrew the tsardom and set up a new model of government.

Founder of the Russian Communist Party, Vladimir Ilich Lenin.

COMMUNISM AND FASCISM

In cold fact, the new Russian government was not quite as new as many of its admirers and enemies believed. Tyranny was as old as civilization itself. Prior tyrannical leaders enacted the belief that society was best governed by the discipline thought necessary in an army at war. Such, too, was the underlying principle of the Soviet Union, though it professed to be a democracy and to be guided by the most advanced and scientific social philosophy of its age.

Vladimir Ilich Lenin and his followers, the Bolsheviks (later known as the Communist Party of the Soviet Union), won power in the turmoil of revolutionary Russia because they were abler and more unscrupulous than any other group. They retained and increased their power by force, but they argued that the theories of Karl Marx (1818–83), as developed by Lenin, were of universal, permanent, and all-sufficient validity, that the leadership of the Communist Party had a unique understanding of those theories and of the proper tactics for realizing them, and that therefore the party's will could never legitimately be resisted.

The Soviet model found many imitators. Lenin's strictly disciplined revolutionary party, the only morality of which was unswerving obedience to the leader, was a particularly attractive example to those intent on seizing power in a world made chaotic by World War I, such as Benito Mussolini of Italy. Adolf Hitler of Germany added a vicious anti-Semitism and a lust for mass murder to that brew. Mao Zedong in China combined Leninism with a hatred of all the foreign imperialists who had reduced China to nullity. In the Soviet Union itself Lenin's successor and disciple, Joseph Stalin, outdid his master in building up his power by mass terror and party discipline.

Terror and technology were all that kept their regimes afloat, yet in their time they undeniably had a certain prestige. Liberal democracy and liberal economics had apparently failed, suggesting to some minds that the future of government lay with totalitarianism. However, after Stalin's death in 1953, the Soviet empire began to lurch from crisis to crisis. In 1985 a new generation came to power under Mikhail Gorbachev, who was willing to take enormous risks in order to revitalize the Soviet empire. Before long, though, the communist regimes in Europe disintegrated, and in 1991 the Soviet Union itself dissolved.

LIBERAL DEMOCRACY

Meanwhile, liberal democracy had gotten its second wind. Although the democracies had failed to avert the World Wars and the Great Depression, they crushed the Axis powers in World War II and warded off the rivalry of communism in the Cold War that followed. The democratic system everywhere brought with it growing prosperity, the emancipation of women, recognition of the equal rights of law-abiding individuals and social groups (whatever their origins or beliefs), and a professed commitment to international cooperation. However, the prosperity of Western democracies, as well as their free markets and free political institutions, was putting enormous strain on the rest of the world, since the West used up far more of the globe's natural and human resources than the size of its population seemed to justify. Non-Western societies were also having to cope with the disproportionate effects of such problems as a rapidly growing population, the HIV/AIDS pandemic, and the worldwide environmental issues of ozone depletion and global warming. It was natural for some, or most, in every country threatened by the hurricane of change to cling, however futilely, to the shreds of tradition, or even to try to rebuild an order that had failed. So it was in much of the Islamic world, where a resurgence of religious fundamentalism led to campaigns for the establishment of Islamic republics, following the example of Iran and the short-lived Taliban regime of Afghanistan. But religious dictatorships did not seem likely to solve modern problems any better than the military or secular kind had done.

PROSPECTS IN THE 21ST CENTURY

In a world increasingly knit together by trade and communications technology, it seems ever more unlikely that the single nation-state can on its own successfully handle the universal enemies of poverty, hunger, disease, natural disaster, and war or other violence. Some thinkers believe that only a form of world government can make decisive headway against those evils, but no one has yet suggested convincingly either how a world government could be set up without another world war or how, if such a government did somehow come peacefully into existence, it could be organized so as to be worthy of its name. Even effective global cooperation among national governments can be extremely difficult, as the examples of the United Nations and other international bodies have shown. Nevertheless, those bodies have had many accomplishments, and the European Union (EU) has been particularly successful. The EU began as an attempt to bury the long-standing rivalry between France and Germany through economic cooperation. By the early 21st century it had come to include almost all the states between the Russian frontier and the Atlantic Ocean. Though its overall constitutional structure remained weak, and agreement on how to sufficiently strengthen it seemed unattainable, the EU's common laws and policies were playing a large part in the lives of its citizens.

Yet Western democracy also faces other problems that may prove too big for it to solve. The great experiment of European imperialism has long since collapsed, but its legacy of corruption, war, and poverty, especially in Africa, seemed even more challenging at the beginning of the 21st century than it did 50 years previously. In all countries, nationalism still distorts voters' judgments in matters of foreign policy, as greed misleads them over economic policy. Class conflicts have been muted rather than resolved. Demagogues abound as much as they did in ancient Athens. The incompatible claims of the city-states ruined ancient Greece; modern civilization may yet be imperiled by the rival claims of the nation-states. At least one thing is clear, however: if human beings, as political animals, are to progress further, they cannot yet rest from seeking new forms of government to meet the ever-new needs of their times.

CHAPTER SEVEN

PUBLIC ADMINISTRATION

Public administration consists of the implementation of government policies. It is a feature of all nations, whatever their system of government. Within nations public administration is practiced at the central, intermediate, and local levels. Indeed, the relationships between different levels of government within a single nation constitute a growing problem of public administration.

EARLY SYSTEMS OF ADMINISTRATION

Public administration has ancient origins. In antiquity the Egyptians and Greeks organized public affairs by office, and the principal officeholders were regarded as being principally responsible for administering justice, maintaining law and order, and providing plenty. The Romans developed a more sophisticated system under their empire, creating distinct administrative hierarchies for justice, military affairs, finance and taxation, foreign affairs, and internal affairs, each with its own principal officers of state. An elaborate administrative structure, later imitated by the Roman Catholic Church, covered the entire empire, with a hierarchy of officers reporting back through their superiors to the emperor. This sophisticated structure disappeared after the fall of the Roman Empire in western Europe in the 5th century, but many of its practices continued in the Byzantine Empire in the east, where civil service rule was reflected in the pejorative use of the word *Byzantinism*.

Early European administrative structures developed from the royal households of the medieval period. Until the end of the 12th century official duties within the royal households were ill-defined, frequently with multiple holders of the same post. Exceptions were the better-defined positions of butler (responsible for the provision of wine), steward (responsible for feasting arrangements), chamberlain (often charged with receiving and paying out money kept in the royal sleeping chamber), and chancellor (usually a priest with responsibilities for writing and applying the seal in the monarch's name). With the 13th century a separation began between the purely domestic functions of the royal household and the functions connected with governing the state. The older household posts tended to disappear, become sinecures, or decline in importance. The office of chancellor, which had always been concerned with matters of state, survived to become the most important link between the old court offices and modern ministries, and the development of the modern treasury or finance ministry can be traced back to the chamberlain's office in the royal household.

From the middle of the 13th century three institutions began to emerge as the major bodies for handling affairs of state: the high court (evolving primarily from the chancellery), the exchequer, and the collegial royal council. In England and France, however, it was not until the early 14th century that such bodies emerged. In Brandenburg, which was governed by an elector (a prince with a right to elect the Holy Roman emperor) and which later formed the basis of the Prussian state, they became distinct entities only at the beginning of the 17th century.

THE SONG/SUNG DYNASTY

The Song dynasty (also called the Sung dynasty) that ruled China from 960–1279 was in power during one of China's most brilliant cultural epochs. It is commonly divided into Bei (Northern) and Nan (Southern) Song periods, as the dynasty ruled only in South China after 1127.

The Bei Song was founded by Zhao Kuangyin, the military inspector general of the Hou (Later) Zhou dynasty (last of the Five Dynasties), who usurped control of the empire in a coup. He persuaded powerful potential rivals to exchange their power for honours and sinecures, and became an admirable emperor (known as Taizu, his temple name). He set the nation on a course of sound administration by instituting a competent and pragmatic civil service; he followed Confucian principles, lived modestly, and took the country's finest military units under his personal command. Before his death he had begun an expansion into the small Ten Kingdoms of southern China.

Taizu's successors maintained an uneasy peace with the menacing Liao kingdom of the Khitan to the north. As the dynasty's bureaucracy deteriorated, they became easy prey. The Juchen took over the North and established a dynasty with a Chinese name, the Jin.

In the South, the climate and the beautiful surroundings were the setting for the Nan Song dynasty established (1127) by the emperor Gaozong. In due course, however, the dynasty began to decline. Their eventual fall was because of a sustained campaign by the Mongols, under Genghis Khan, who began with an assault on the Jin state in the North in 1211 and ended with Genghis Khan's grandsons who fought on until 1276, when the Song capital fell. The dynasty finally ended in 1279 with the destruction of the Song fleet near Guangzhou (Canton).

Apart from justice and treasury departments, which originated in old court offices, modern ministerial structures in Europe developed out of the royal councils, which were powerful bodies of nobles appointed by the monarch. From the division of labour within these bodies the monarchs' secretaries, initially given low status within a council, emerged as perhaps the first professional civil servants in Europe in the modern sense. The proximity of the secretaries to the monarch gave them more knowledge of royal intentions, and their relative permanence gave them greater expertise in particular matters of state than could be found among the more transient nobles on the council. They were also assisted by staffs. The secretaries grew in importance in the 15th and 16th centuries as they became more or less full members of the council.

The distribution of functions among secretaries was initially based upon geography. In England this geographical allocation—with, for example, a secretary of the North and a secretary of the South—persisted until 1782, when the offices of home and foreign secretary were created. In France a more complex allocation of territorial responsibilities among secretaries of state had begun to give way to functional responsibilities by the end of the ancien régime in 1789.

The civil service in China was undoubtedly the longest lasting in history; it was first organized, along with a centralized administration, during the Han dynasty (206 BC–AD 220) and improved under the T'ang (618–907) and Song (960–1279). The administration was organized so well that the pattern stood until 1912. During the Song dynasty there developed the full use of civil service examinations. Candidates were subjected to successive elimination through written tests on three levels, more than a hundred persons beginning the ordeal for each one who emerged successful. Although there was strong emphasis on the Chinese Classics (because knowledge of the Classics was thought to form the virtues of a good citizen), there was also an effort to devise objective and meaningful tests for practical qualities, and there were always long contentions over subject matter and testing methods. To preserve the anonymity of the candidate and to ensure fairness in grading, examination papers were copied by clerks, examinees were identified by number only, and three examiners read each paper. Higher officials were privileged to nominate junior relatives for admission to the bureaucracy, but the great stress on examination grades in promotion, the use of annual merit ratings, and the practice of recruiting many lower officials from the ranks of the clerical service ensured a considerable freedom of opportunity.

MODERN DEVELOPMENTS

The modernization of government continued throughout the developed world. Specific civil positions became defined regardless of political system. Some countries emphasized centralization, while developing countries struggled for consistency.

PRUSSIA

The foundations of modern public administration in Europe were laid in Prussia in the late 17th and 18th centuries. The electors of Brandenburg considered a rigidly centralized government a means of ensuring stability and furthering dynastic objectives. Their principal effort was devoted in the first instance to the suppression of the autonomy of the cities and to the elimination of the feudal privileges of the aristocracy. Civil servants were therefore appointed by the central government to administer the provinces, where the management of crown lands and the organization of the military system were combined in a Kriegs-und-Domänen-kammer ("Office of War and Crown Lands"). Subordinate to these offices were the *Steuerräte* ("tax councillors"), who controlled the administration of the municipalities and communes. These officials were all appointed by the central government and were responsible to it. At the apex of the new machinery of government was the sovereign.

This centralized system was strengthened by creating a special corps of civil servants. Special ordinances in 1722 and 1748 regulated recruitment to the civil service. A single General Code regularized the system of recruitment, promotion, and internal organization in 1794. Entry to the higher civil service required a university degree in cameralistics, which was the science of public finance and included the study of administrative law, police administration, estate management, and agricultural economics. After the degree course, candidates for the higher civil service spent a further period of supervised practical training in various branches of the administration, at the end of which they underwent a further oral and written examination. The basic principles of modern civil services are to be found in this General Code.

FRANCE

A fundamental change in the status of the civil servant came about as a result of the French Revolution of 1789. The fall of the ancien régime and the creation of a republic meant that the civil servant was seen as the servant no longer of the king but rather of the state—even though rule by a king or emperor was soon brought back and continued in France for nearly another century. The civil servant became an instrument of public power, not the agent of a person.

Bureaucratization was greatly fostered by Napoleon I, who built up a new civil service marked not only by some of the features of military organization but also by the principles of rationality, logic, and universality that were the inheritance of the Enlightenment. There was a clear chain of command and a firmly established hierarchy of officials, with duties clearly apportioned between authorities. Civil servants had a general responsibility for maintaining public order, health, and morality. They were all linked in a chain to the national Ministry of the Interior. A special school, the École Polytechnique, was set up to provide the state with technical specialists in both the military and the civil fields—particularly in general administration.

In France under the Third Republic (1870–1940) there developed, however, considerable political interference in some branches of the civil service; and much of its vitality was diminished as its bureaucratic practices tended to become unwieldy and its personnel lethargic. Not until 1946 was the system reformed—which involved overhauling the administrative structure of the central government, centralizing personnel selection, creating a special ministry for civil service affairs, and setting up a special school, the École National d'Administration, for the training of senior civil servants.

THE BRITISH EMPIRE

The first attempts by Great Britain to create efficient administrative machinery arose from its commitment to govern India. Robert Clive, appointed governor of Bengal for the second time in 1764, introduced a code of practice that prohibited servants of the East India Company from trading on their own account or accepting gifts from native traders. Recruitment was carried on by the company in London, and after 1813 entrants to the civil service had to study the history, language, and laws of India for a period of four terms at Haileybury College, England, and to obtain a certificate of good conduct before taking up their posts. New rules from 1833 stipulated that four candidates had to be nominated for each vacancy and that they were to compete with one another in "an examination in such branches of knowledge and by such examinations as the Board of the Company shall direct."

In 1853 another legislative reform of the administration was proposed. The experience of the Indian Civil Service influenced the foundation of the modern civil service in the United Kingdom. A report of 1854 recommended the abolition of patronage and recruitment by open competitive examination. It further recommended (1) the establishment of an autonomous semijudicial body of civil service commissioners to ensure the proper administration of recruitment to official posts, (2) the division of the work of the civil service into intellectual and routine

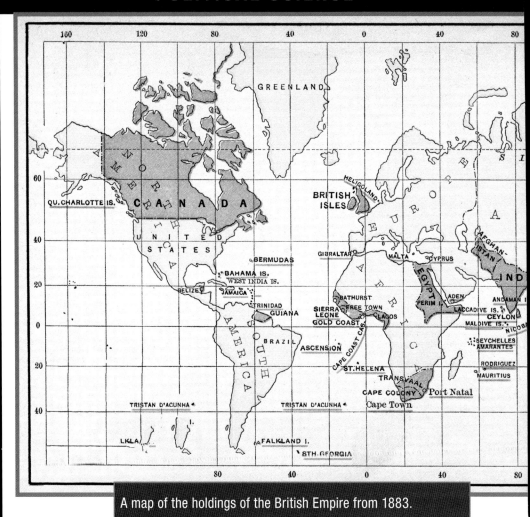

A map of the holdings of the British Empire from 1883.

work, the two sets of offices to have separate forms of recruitment, and (3) the selection of higher civil servants more decidedly on the basis of general intellectual attainment than specialized knowledge. The Civil Service Commission was established in 1855, and during the next 30 years patronage was gradually eliminated. The two original classes were increased to four, and some specialized branches were amalgamated to become the Scientific Civil Service. The new civil service managed to

attract to its senior levels highly capable, discreet, and self-effacing university graduates.

THE UNITED STATES

In the United States patronage remained the norm for considerably longer than in Britain. From the early days of the federation two principles were firmly held. First, there was antipathy to the notion of a cadre of permanent civil servants. The second principle held that as far as possible public office should be elective. After the Civil War, the federal government accepted a restricted principle of entry by competitive open examination, and in 1883 the U.S. Civil Service Commission was established to control entry to office in the federal service. After 1978 the functions of the commission were divided between the Office of Personnel Management and the Merit Systems Protection Board. Principal policy-making posts, numbering some 2,000, remain outside the jurisdiction of these two bodies, being filled instead by presidential nomination.

The development of civil service in U.S. local government varied among states, counties, and cities. The adoption of a merit system can usually be dated from the early 20th century, during the reform period of the muckrakers. In some states the merit system became well established, with a central personnel office that included a civil service commission or board similar to the federal model. At the other extreme there was simply a central personnel office headed by a single personnel director with no advisory board. At the municipal level, by the mid-20th century, most large cities in the United States had developed some sort of merit system; in smaller cities, however, merit systems were correspondingly less common. In the counties, the majority of which were rural and had relatively few public employees, formally established merit systems were rare.

THE SOVIET UNION

In Russia the Revolution of 1917 swept away the tsarist civil service. The Communist Party at first held that a strong administrative organization was bound to damage the revolution by dampening spontaneity and other revolutionary virtues. But it soon became clear that a regime dedicated to social engineering, economic planning, and world revolution needed trained administrators.

As the Communist Party itself became bureaucratized and as the more enthusiastic revolutionary leaders were eliminated, special industrial academies were set up for party members who had shown administrative talent. With the First Five-Year Plan (1928–32) the conditions of service and status of civil servants was improved. In 1935 the State Commission on the Civil Service was created and attached to the Commissariat of Finance with responsibility for ensuring general control of personnel practice. This commission remained under the close supervision of the Council of People's Commissars to ensure that it complied with party directives, but unlike those in such countries as Great Britain and the United States, was given no jurisdiction over the recruitment of civil servants. The Communist Party made determined attempts to recruit higher civil servants as party members. These drives, which followed periodically after the 1930s, went a long way toward transforming the party itself into an administrative and managerial elite and uniting the party and the state administration.

CHINA

The People's Republic of China also illustrates the conflict between revolutionary suspicion of bureaucracy and the need to construct strong administrative machinery in order to attain revolutionary goals. China's long tradition of bureaucracy remained important even after the Communist Party came to power in 1949. Within a decade the weight of the administration had already led, according to party dogma, to a gap between the elite and the masses and also to excessive stratification among the ruling bureaucrats, or cadres, themselves. There was not only a distinction between "old cadres" and "new cadres," depending on nothing more substantial than the date of an official's entry into the revolutionary movement, but also a complex system of job evaluation that divided the civil service into 24 grades, each with its own rank, salary scales, and distinctions. The number of ratings represented very considerable differences of power, prestige, and prerogatives and produced psychological barriers between the highest and lowest grades at least as great and as conspicuous as between the cadres and the masses. These distinctions and discrepancies were widely attacked during the Cultural Revolution of the 1960s and '70s, but they remained deeply ingrained in the administrative structure.

JAPAN

Until the 17th century, Japan under the shogunate was administered by a military establishment made up of vassals and enfeoffed nobles. After the 1630s a civil bureaucracy developed and began to assume a more important role than the military. Appointment within the bureaucracy was based upon family rank, and officials were loyal primarily to the feudal lord. Japanese bureaucracy moved away from feudal rank as the basis of appointments only after Matthew C. Perry sailed four U.S. warships into Uraga, ending Japan's isolation from the rest of the world. During the Meiji Restoration of the 1880s a modern civil service was created on the basis of job security, career paths, and entry by open competition.

After World War II the Allied occupation authorities directed the passage of a Japanese law guaranteeing that all public officials should be servants of the people rather than of the emperor. The National Public Service Law of 1947 set up an independent National Personnel Authority to administer recruitment, promotion, conditions of employment, standards of performance, and job classification for the new civil service. Technically the emperor himself became a civil servant, and detailed regulations brought within the scope of the new law all civil servants from labourers to the prime minister. Civil servants were classified into two groups, the regular service and a special service. Civil servants in the former category entered the service by competitive examination on a standard contract with tenure. The special service included elected officials and political appointees and covered such officials as members of the Diet (legislature), judges, members of the audit boards, and ambassadors.

DEVELOPING NATIONS

Less-developed countries have had to face the opposite problem with their civil services. After World War II many such countries became independent before they had developed effective administrative structures or bodies of trained civil servants. Few of the colonial powers had trained indigenous administrators sufficiently. The British left a viable administrative structure in India and a partly Indianized civil service, but the newly independent Pakistan had few experienced civil servants. The Belgians left the Congo without any trained administrative or technical staff, and for some years there was near anarchy.

Even when they inherited reasonably efficient administrative organizations, the newly independent countries' politicians frequently proved incapable of fulfilling their supporters' expectations. Civil servants from the old colonial powers who remained behind often found radical

Soldiers in an independence day parade in the former British colony Trinidad and Tobago.

policies and new masters uncongenial. The resulting exodus of many such civil servants worsened matters, for indigenous civil servants were seldom an adequate substitute.

The lack of qualified personnel sometimes led to not only a reduction in efficiency but also a decline in administrative morality. Nepotism, tribalism, and corruption as well as inefficiency in the civil service were difficulties often added to the other trials of independence. In many countries the incapacity of the civil service was a factor leading to military rule, as were the political failings of the elected leaders. Military regimes have frequently been the last resort of a country where the civil power has failed to cope with the problems of independence.

Consequently, the United Nations (UN), in conjunction with the governments of advanced countries, began to develop training programs for civil servants from underdeveloped countries. The first request came from Latin America, which led to the founding of a school of public administration in Brazil, followed in 1953 by an Advanced School of Public Administration for Central America. Various other international organizations, including the Organisation for Economic Co-operation and Development and the World Bank, supported institutions for the training of administrators in the less-developed countries. Such institutions included the Arab Planning Institute in Kuwait, the Arab Organization of Administrative Sciences in Jordan, and the Inter-American School of Public Administration in Brazil. Civil servants from the less-developed nations also studied administration at such places as the Institute of Social Studies in The Hague, Neth., the Institute of Local Government Studies in Birmingham, Eng., and the International Institute of Public Administration in Paris.

After the 1970s the international agencies gave less help toward training, on the assumption—often unrealized—that the less-developed nations would take on greater responsibility themselves. Training also tended to be generalist and academic, leading to acute shortages of trained administrators in specialized fields such as finance and planning. However, organizations such as the British Council began in the early 1980s to remedy some of these deficiencies.

CHAPTER EIGHT

CONSTITUTIONAL GOVERNMENT

Aconstitution is the body of doctrines and practices that form the fundamental organizing principle of a political state. In some cases, such as the United States, the constitution is a specific written document; in others, such as the United Kingdom, it is a collection of documents, statutes, and traditional practices that are generally accepted as governing political matters. States that have a written constitution may also have a body of traditional or customary practices that may or may not be considered to be of constitutional standing. Virtually every state claims to have a constitution, but not every government conducts itself in a consistently constitutional manner.

The general idea of a constitution and of constitutionalism originated with the ancient Greeks and especially in the systematic, theoretical, normative, and descriptive writings of Aristotle. In his *Politics, Nicomachean Ethics, Constitution of Athens,* and other works, Aristotle used the Greek word for constitution (*politeia*) in several different senses. The simplest and most neutral of these was "the arrangement of the offices in a polis" (state). In this purely descriptive sense of the word, every state has a constitution, no matter how badly or erratically governed it may be.

FEATURES OF CONSTITUTIONAL GOVERNMENT

Virtually all contemporary governments have constitutions, but possession and publication of a constitution does not make a govern-

Article I of the U.S. Constitution.

ment constitutional. Constitutional government in fact comprises the following elements.

PROCEDURAL STABILITY

Certain fundamental procedures must not be subject to frequent or arbitrary change. Citizens must know the basic rules according to which politics are conducted. Stable procedures of government provide citizens with adequate knowledge of the probable consequences of their actions. By contrast, under many nonconstitutional regimes, such as Hitler's in Germany and Stalin's in the Soviet Union, individuals, including high government officials, never knew from one day to the next whether the whim of the dictator's will would not turn today's hero into tomorrow's public enemy.

ACCOUNTABILITY

Under constitutional government, those who govern are regularly accountable to at least a portion of the governed. In a constitutional democracy, this accountability is owed to the electorate by all persons in government. Accountability can be enforced through a great variety of regular procedures, including elections, systems of promotion and discipline, fiscal accounting, recall, and referendum. In constitutional democracies, the accountability of government officials *to* the citizenry makes possible the citizens' responsibility *for* the acts of government. The most obvious example of this two-directional flow of responsibility and accountability is the electoral process. A member of the legislature or the head of government is elected by adult citizens and is thereby invested with authority and power in order that he may try to achieve those goals to which he committed himself in his program. At the end of his term of office, the electorate has the opportunity to judge his performance and to reelect him or dismiss him from office. The official has thus rendered his account and has been held accountable.

REPRESENTATION

Those in office must conduct themselves as the representatives of their constituents. To represent means to be present on behalf of someone else who is absent. Elections, of course, are not the only means of securing representation or of ensuring the representativeness of a government. Hereditary medieval kings considered themselves, and were generally considered by their subjects, to be representatives of their societies. Of the social contract theorists only Rousseau denied the feasibility of representation for purposes of legislation. The elected status of officeholders is sometimes considered no guarantee that they will be "existentially representative" of their constituents, unless they share with the latter certain other vital characteristics such as race, religion, sex, or age. The problems of representation are in fact more closely related to democratic than to constitutionalist criteria of government: a regime that would be considered quite unrepresentative by modern standards could still be regarded as constitutional so long as it provided procedural stability and the accountability of officeholders to some but not all of the governed and so long as the governors were representative of the best or the most important elements in the body politic.

DIVISION OF POWER

Constitutional government requires a division of power among several organs of the body politic. Preconstitutionalist governments, such as the absolute monarchies of Europe in the 18th century, frequently concentrated all power in the hands of a single person. The same has been true in modern dictatorships such as Hitler's in Germany. Constitutionalism, on the other hand, by dividing power—between, for example, local and central government and between the legislature, executive, and judiciary—ensures the presence of restraints and "checks and balances" in the political system. Citizens are thus able to influence policy by resort to any of several branches of government.

OPENNESS AND DISCLOSURE

Democracy rests upon popular participation in government, constitutionalism upon disclosure of and openness about the affairs of government. In this sense, constitutionalism is a prerequisite of successful democracy, since the people cannot participate rationally in government unless they are adequately informed of its workings. Originally, because they were concerned with secrets of state, bureaucracies surrounded their activities with a veil of secrecy. The ruler himself always retained full access to administrative secrets and often to the private affairs of his subjects, into which bureaucrats such as tax collectors and the police could legally pry. But when both administrators and rulers were subjected to constitutional restraints, it became necessary that they disclose the content of their official activities to the public to which they owed accountability. This explains the provision contained in most constitutions obliging the legislature to publish a record of its debates.

CONSTITUTIONALITY

Written constitutions normally provide the standard by which the legitimacy of governmental actions is judged. In the United States, the practice of the judicial review of congressional legislation for its constitutionality—that is, for its conformity with the U.S. Constitution—though not explicitly provided for by the Constitution, developed in the early years of the republic. More recently, other written constitutions, including the Basic Law of the Federal Republic of Germany and Italy's republican constitution, provided explicitly for judicial review of the constitutionality of parliamentary legislation. This does not necessarily mean that a constitution is regarded as being prior and superior to all law. Although several European countries, including France and Italy, adopted new constitutions after World War II, they kept in force their codes of civil law, which had been legislated in the 19th century; and the U.S. Constitution guarantees citizens certain substantive and procedural rights to which they deemed themselves entitled as subjects of the British crown under the ancient English common law. Despite the greater antiquity of law codes, however, portions of them have been revised from time to time in order to eliminate conflicts between the law and certain constitutional norms that are regarded as superior. Parts of German family law and of the criminal code, for example, were revised in order to bring them into conformity with the constitutional provisions regarding the equality of persons irrespective of sex and with the individual's constitutionally guaranteed right to the free development of his personality.

Conflicting interests or parties are, of course, likely to place different interpretations on particular provisions of a constitution, and means, therefore, have to be provided for the resolution of such conflicts. The constitution itself may establish an institution, the task of which is to interpret and clarify the terms of that constitution. In the American system, the Supreme Court is generally regarded as the authoritative interpreter of the Constitution. But the Supreme Court cannot be regarded as the "final" interpreter of the meaning of the Constitution for a number of reasons. The court can always reverse itself, as it has done before. The president can gradually change the interpretative outlook of the court through the nomination of new justices, and the Congress can exert a more negative influence by refusing to confirm presidential nominations of justices.

Provision was made in the constitution of the Fifth French Republic for the interpretation of certain constitutional matters by a Constitutional Council. Soon after the French electorate, in a referendum in 1958, had voted to accept the Constitution, a controversy erupted in France over the question of whether the president of the republic could submit to popular referendum issues not involving constitutional amendments but on which parliament had taken a position at odds with the president's. The Constitution itself seemed to provide that the Constitutional Council could rule definitively on this question, but Pres. Charles de Gaulle chose to ignore its ruling, which was unfavourable to himself. As a result, the Constitutional Council lost authority as the final interpreter of the meaning of the Constitution of the Fifth Republic.

It may thus be seen that because of the inherent difficulties in assessing the intentions of the authors of a constitution and because of the possibility that the executive or legislative branch of government may be able to ignore, override, or influence its findings, it is difficult to ensure constitutional government merely by setting up an institution whose purpose is constitutional interpretation.

CONSTITUTIONAL CHANGE

Written constitutions are not only likely to give rise to greater problems of interpretation than unwritten ones, but they are also harder to change. Unwritten constitutions tend to change gradually, continually, and often imperceptibly, in response to changing needs. But when a constitution lays down exact procedures for the election of the president, for relations between the executive and legislative branches, or for defining whether a particular governmental function is to be performed by the federal government or a member state, then the only constitutional way to change these procedures is by means of the procedure provided by the constitution itself for its own amendment. Any attempt to effect change by means of judicial review or interpretation is unconstitutional, unless, of course, the constitution provides that a body (such as the U.S. Supreme Court) may change, rather than interpret, the constitution.

Many constitutional documents make no clear distinction between that which is to be regarded as constitutional, fundamental, and organic, on the one hand, and that which is merely legislative, circumstantial, and more or less transitory, on the other. The constitution of the German Weimar Republic could be amended by as little as four-ninths of the membership of the Reichstag, without any requirement for subsequent ratification by the states, by constitutional conventions, or by referendum. Although Hitler never explicitly abrogated the Weimar Constitution, he was able to replace the procedural and institutional stability that it had sought to establish with a condition of almost total procedural and institutional flux.

A similar situation prevailed in the Soviet Union under the rule of Stalin. But Stalin took great trouble and some pride in having a constitution bearing his name adopted in 1936. The Stalin constitution continued, together with the Rules of the Communist Party of the Soviet Union, to serve as the formal framework of government until the ratification of a new, though rather similar, constitution in 1977. The procedures established by these documents, however, were not able to provide Soviet citizens and politicians with reliable knowledge of the rules of the political process from one year to the next or with guidance as to which institutions and practices they were to consider fundamental or virtually sacrosanct and which they could safely criticize. As a result, changes in the personnel and policies of the Soviet Union and of similar Communist regimes were rarely brought about smoothly and frequently required the use of violence.

CONSTITUTIONAL STABILITY

If one distinguishes between stability and stagnation on the one hand and between flexibility and flux on the other, then one can consider those constitutional systems most successful that combine procedural stability with substantive flexibility—that is, that preserve the same general rules of political procedure from one generation to the next while at the same time facilitating adaptation to changing circumstances. By reference to such criteria, those written constitutions have achieved the greatest success that are comparatively short; that confine themselves in the main to matters of procedure (including their own amendment) rather than matters of substance; that, to the extent that they contain substantive provisions at all, keep these rather vague and generalized; and that contain procedures that are congruent with popular political experience and know-how. These general characteristics appear to be more important in making for stability than such particular arrangements as the relations between various organs and levels of government or the powers, functions, and terms of tenure of different officers of state.

There is little evidence to support the thesis that a high level of citizen participation necessarily contributes to the stability of constitutional government. On the contrary, the English political economist Walter Bagehot, who in 1867 wrote a classic analysis of the English constitution (*The English Constitution*), stressed the "deferential" character of the English people, who were quite happy to leave government in the hands of the governing class.

Much more important than formal citizen behaviour, such as electoral participation, are informal attitudes and practices and the extent to which they are congruent with the formal prescriptions and proscriptions of the constitution itself. Constitutional government cannot survive effectively in situations in which the constitution prescribes a pattern of behaviour or of conducting affairs that is alien to the customs and way of thinking of the people. When, as happened in many developing countries in the decades after World War II, a new and alien kind of constitutional democracy is imposed or adopted, a gap may soon develop between constitutionally prescribed and actual governmental practice. This in turn renders the government susceptible to attack by opposition groups. Such attack is especially easy to mount in situations in which a constitution has a heavy and detailed substantive content, when, for example, it guarantees the right to gainful employment or the right to a university education for all qualified candidates. In the event of the government being unable to fulfill its commitment, the opposition is able to call the constitution a mere scrap of paper and to demand its improvement or even its complete replacement. Such tactics often have succeeded, but they ignore the dual strategic function of the constitution. It is meant not only to arrange the offices of the state, in Aristotle's sense, but also to state the goals toward which the authors and ratifiers of the constitution want their community to move.

THE PRACTICE OF CONSTITUTIONAL GOVERNMENT

Constitutional government as a political system has roots in Great Britain before spreading across the globe.

GREAT BRITAIN

It is accepted constitutional theory that Parliament (the House of Commons and the House of Lords acting with the assent of the monarch) can do anything it wants to, including abolish itself. The interesting aspect of British government is that, despite the absence of restraints such as judicial review, acts that would be considered unconstitutional in the presence of a written constitution are attempted very rarely, certainly less often than in the United States.

Queen Elizabeth II at the opening of Parliament, May 8, 2013.

The locus of power in the English constitution shifted gradually as a result of changes in the groups whose consent the government required in order to be effective. In feudal times, the consent of the great landowning noblemen was needed. Later, the cooperation of commoners willing to grant revenue to the crown—that is, to pay taxes—was sought. The crown itself, meanwhile, was increasingly institutionalized, and the distinction was drawn ever more clearly between the private and public capacities of the king. During the course of the 18th century, effective government passed more and more into the hands of the king's first minister and his cabinet, all of them members of one of the two houses of Parliament. Before this development, the king's ministers depended upon their royal master's confidence to continue in office. Henceforward they depended upon the confidence of the House of Lords and especially the House of Commons, which had to vote the money without which the king's government could not be carried on. In this way the parlay that was originally between the monarch and the houses of Parliament was now struck between the ministry and its supporters, on the one hand, and opposing members of Parliament, on the other. Parliamentary factions were slowly consolidated into parliamentary parties, and these parties reached out for support into the population at large by means of the franchise, which was repeatedly enlarged in the course of the 19th century and eventually extended to women and then to 18-year-olds in the 20th.

When a prime minister loses a vote of confidence in the House of Commons, he can either resign to let the leader of the Opposition form a new government or ask the monarch to dissolve Parliament and call for new elections. As a result of the strong party discipline that developed in the 20th century, prime ministers generally do not lose votes of confidence any more, and they call for new elections at the politically most favourable moment. According to an act of Parliament, elections must be held at least every five years—but another act of Parliament can change or suspend this apparently "constitutional" provision, as was done during World War II, when the life of the incumbent House of Commons was extended until the defeat of Germany. Similarly, relations between, and the relative powers of, the House of Lords and the House of Commons have been repeatedly redefined to the disadvantage of the House of Lords by acts of Parliament, to such an extent that the Lords retain only a weak suspensory veto. All such fundamental constitutional changes have occurred either informally and without any kind of legislation at all or as a result of the same legislative procedures employed to pass any other ordinary circumstantial bill.

UNITED STATES

The U.S. Constitution is not only replete with phrases taken from the British constitutional vocabulary, but in several respects, it also represents a codification of its authors' understanding of the English constitution, to which they added ingenious federalist inventions and the formal amending procedure itself. Despite the availability of this procedure, however, many if not most of the fundamental changes in American constitutional practice have not been effected by formal amendments. The Constitution still does not mention political parties or the president's cabinet. Nor was the Constitution changed in order to bring about or to sanction the fundamentally altered relations between the executive and the Congress, between the Senate and the House, and between the judiciary, the legislature, and the executive.

The presence of a constitutional document, however, has made American politics more consciously "constitutionalist," at least in the sense that politicians in the United States take more frequent recourse than their British counterparts to legalistic argumentation and to actual constitutional litigation. The United States, moreover, is denied the kind of flexibility illustrated by the postponement of British parliamentary elections during World War II since the Constitution explicitly provides the dates for congressional and presidential elections. It is one of the remarkable facts of American constitutional history that the constitutional timetable for elections has always been observed, even during external war and the Civil War of the 19th century.

EUROPE

France, Germany, and Italy, as well as most non-European countries influenced by continental concepts of constitutionalism, have no record of unbroken constitutional fidelity similar to that found in Britain and the

United States. Because of the highly substantive and ideological content of most French constitutions, the best way to change them has been to replace them altogether with a new, ideologically different document. Only the constitution of the Third Republic (established in 1870) was exceptional in this respect, since it consisted of very short, highly procedural organic laws, which served France well for 70 years, until the German invasion of 1940.

The main political problem attributed to the constitution of the Third Republic was the instability of cabinets. The negative majorities that voted "no confidence" in a cabinet usually could not stay together for the positive purpose of confirming a new cabinet. The constitution of the Fourth Republic (1946–58) made the overthrow of governments by the National Assembly more difficult. In fact, however, the life of the average cabinet in the Fourth Republic was even shorter than in the Third, and French government became virtually paralyzed when it had to deal with the problems raised by the Algerian independence movement. To avert a military takeover, General de Gaulle was given wide discretion in 1958 in the formulation of a new constitution, which was overwhelmingly accepted in a referendum. The constitution of the Fifth French Republic gives the president of the Republic the power to dissolve Parliament and the means of circumventing a hostile National Assembly through the referendum. Since 1958, French cabinets have been very stable indeed, and the constitution proved resilient during the student revolt and general strike of May 1968.

Germany, which was unified as a national state only in 1871, established its first democratic constitution in 1919, after its defeat in World War I. Although some of the greatest German jurists and social scientists of the time participated in writing the Weimar Constitution, it has been adjudged a failure. Political parties became highly fragmented, a phenomenon that was explained partly by an extremely democratic electoral law (not a part of the constitution) providing for proportional representation. Some of the parties of the right, such as Hitler's Nazis, and of the left, such as the Communists, were opposed to the constitutional order

British Decolonization and Emerging National Constitutions

The period 1957–62 was also the climax of decolonization. As early as 1946–47, when Britain was granting independence to India and states of the Middle East, the Attlee government sponsored the Cohen–Caine plan for a new approach to West Africa as well. It aimed at preparing tropical Africa for self-rule by gradually transferring local authority from tribal chiefs to members of the Western-educated elite. Accordingly, the Colonial Office drafted elaborate constitutions, most of which had little relevance to real conditions in countries that had no natural boundaries, no ethnic unity or sense of nationalism, and no civic tradition. When the Gold Coast (Ghana) elected the radical leader Kwame Nkrumah, who then demanded immediate independence and got it in 1957, the British felt unable to deny similar grants to neighbouring colonies. In 1959 the Cabinet quietly decided to withdraw from Africa as soon as it won reelection.

Most new African states had little more to support their pretensions to nationhood than a paper constitution, a flag, and a London-backed currency. Africa's politicians invariably styled themselves as charismatic leaders whose political and even spiritual guidance was the prerequisite for progress. Many seized power, which led to military unrest. By 1967 black Africa had suffered 64 attempted coups d'état, many born of tribal hatreds, and most Africans had fewer political rights than under colonial rule.

and used violence in their efforts to overthrow the Republic. To deal with these threats, the president used his constitutional emergency powers under which he could suspend civil rights in member states of the federal system. Several chancellors (the German equivalent of a prime minister) stayed in office after the president had dissolved a Parliament in which the chancellor lacked a supporting majority. They continued to govern with the help of presidential emergency powers and by legislating on the basis of powers previously delegated to them by Parliament.

When a new constitution was drafted for the Western zones of occupation after World War II, every effort was made to correct those constitutional errors to which the failure of the Weimar Republic was attributed. Under the Basic Law of the Federal Republic of Germany, Parliament cannot delegate its legislative function to the chancellor, and civil rights cannot be suspended without continuous parliamentary surveillance. The president has been turned into a figurehead on the model of the French presidents of the Third and Fourth Republics, and Parliament cannot overthrow a chancellor and his cabinet unless it first elects a successor with the vote of a majority of its members. Negative majorities cannot paralyze government unless they can agree on alternative policies and personnel. The extreme form of proportional representation used before Hitler came to power was replaced by a mixed electoral system under which half the members of the Bundestag (the lower house of the legislature) are elected from party lists by proportional representation, while the other half are elected in single member constituencies. In order to benefit from proportional representation, a party must obtain at least 5 percent of the votes cast. As a result, the number of parties steadily contracted during the first two decades of the Federal Republic and extremist parties were kept out of Parliament. Cabinets have been very stable, and the provision for the "constructive vote of no confidence" was invoked for the first time only in 1982.

Kwame Nkrumah, the first president of Ghana.

LATIN AMERICA, AFRICA, AND ASIA

The experience of constitutional government in continental Europe exerted great influence on the newly independent former colonies of Europe in the Middle East, Asia, and Africa. In the early years of their independence from Spain, most Latin-American countries adopted constitutions similar to that of the United States. But since they lacked the background that produced the American Constitution, including English common law, most of their efforts at constitutional engineering were unsuccessful.

In Asia and Africa and in the Caribbean, many former colonies of Great Britain, such as India, Nigeria, Zambia, and Jamaica, have been comparatively more successful in the operation of constitutional government than former colonies of the continental European countries (*e.g.,* Indonesia, Congo, and Haiti). The British usually left a modified and simplified version of their own constitution upon granting independence to their former subjects, some of whom they had previously trained in the complicated operating procedures of the British constitution. British parliamentary procedure proved sufficiently adaptable to remain in use for some time after the departure of the British themselves. France's former colonies in Africa, because they achieved independence after the founding of the Fifth Republic, modeled their new constitutions upon General de Gaulle's, partly because this enhanced the power of the leaders under whom independence had been achieved.

CHAPTER NINE

INFLUENTIAL FIGURES IN POLITICAL SCIENCE

The thinkers and scholars discussed in this chapter have made historically important contributions to the development of political science.

CONFUCIUS

(551–479 BCE)

Confucius was born in Qufu in the small feudal state of Lu in what is now Shandong province. His family name was Kong and his personal name Qiu, but he is referred to as either Kongzi or Kongfuzi (Master Kong) throughout Chinese history. Confucius had served in minor government posts managing stables and keeping books for granaries before he married a woman of similar background when he was 19. Confucius is known as the first teacher in China who wanted to make education broadly available and who was instrumental in establishing the art of teaching as a vocation. For Confucius the primary function of education was to provide the proper way of training exemplary persons (*junzi*), a process that involved constant self-improvement and continuous social interaction.

Confucius, China's most famous teacher, philosopher, and political theorist.

In his late 40s and early 50s Confucius served first as a magistrate, then as an assistant minister of public works, and eventually as minister of justice in the state of Lu. It is likely that he accompanied King Lu as his chief minister on one of the diplomatic missions. Confucius's political career was, however, short-lived. His loyalty to the king alienated him from the power holders of the time, the large Ji families, and his moral rectitude did not sit well with the king's inner circle, who enraptured the king with sensuous delight. At 56, when he realized that his superiors were uninterested in his policies, Confucius left the country in an attempt to find another feudal state to which he could render his service. Despite his political frustration he was accompanied by an expanding circle of students during this self-imposed exile of almost 12 years. His reputation as a man of vision and mission spread.

At the age of 67 he returned home to teach and to preserve his cherished classical traditions by writing and editing. He died in 479 BCE, at the age of 73.

PLATO

(428/427–348/347 BCE)

Plato was an ancient Greek philosopher, student of Socrates (c. 470–399 BCE), teacher of Aristotle (384–322 BCE), and founder of the Academy, and is best known as the author of philosophical works of unparalleled influence. Plato's family was aristocratic and distinguished: his father's side claimed descent from the god Poseidon, and his mother's side was related to the lawgiver Solon (c. 630–560 BCE). Plato as a young man was a member of the circle around Socrates. The works of Plato commonly referred to as "Socratic" represent the sort of thing the historical Socrates was doing. He would challenge men who supposedly had expertise about some facet of human excellence to give accounts of these matters—variously of courage, piety, and so on, or at times of the whole of "virtue"—and they typically failed to maintain their position. Resentment against Socrates grew, leading ultimately to his trial and execution.

After the death of Socrates, Plato may have traveled extensively in Greece, Italy, and Egypt. Plato, at Dion's urging, apparently undertook to put into practice the ideal of the "philosopher-king" (described in Plato's dialogue the *Republic*) by educating Dionysius the Younger; the project was not a success, and in the ensuing instability Dion was murdered. Plato's Academy, founded in the 380s, was the ultimate ancestor of the modern university (hence the English term *academic*); an influential centre of research and learning, it attracted many men of outstanding ability.

In the *Republic,* the character Socrates undertakes to show what Justice is and why it is in each person's best interest to be just. Socrates develops the proposal that Justice in a city or an individual is the condition in which each part performs the task that is proper to it; such an entity will have no motivation to do unjust acts and will be free of internal conflict. The middle books of the *Republic* contain a sketch of Plato's views on knowledge and reality and feature the famous figures of the Sun and the Cave, among others.

ARISTOTLE

(384–322 BCE)

Aristotle was an ancient Greek philosopher and scientist, one of the greatest intellectual figures of Western history. He was the author of a philosophical and scientific system that became the framework and vehicle for both Christian Scholasticism and medieval Islamic philosophy.

Aristotle was born on the Chalcidic peninsula of Macedonia, in northern Greece. He was a pupil and colleague of Plato's for 20 years. When Plato died about 348, Aristotle left Athens. He eventually became tutor to Philip II's 13-year-old son, the future Alexander the Great, though their relationship cooled in later years. While Alexander was conquering Asia, Aristotle, now 50 years old, established his own school in a gymnasium known as the Lyceum.

Aristotle famously observed that "Man is a political animal": human beings are creatures of flesh and blood, rubbing shoulders with each other in cities and communities. Aristotle's political studies combine observation and theory. He and his students documented the constitutions of 158 states—one of which, The Constitution of Athens, has survived on papyrus. Aristotle asserts that all communities aim at some good. The state (polis), by which he means a city-state such as Athens, is the highest kind of community, aiming at the highest of goods. Government, Aristotle says, must be in the hands of one, of a few, or of the many; and governments may govern for the general good or for the good of the rulers. Government by a single person for the general good is called monarchy; for private benefit, tyranny. Government by a minority is aristocracy if it aims at the state's best interest and oligarchy if it benefits only the ruling minority. Popular government in the common interest Aristotle calls polity; he reserves the word *democracy* for anarchic mob rule.

KAUTILYA

(Flourished 300 BCE)

Kautilya was a Hindu statesman and philosopher who wrote a classic treatise on polity, *Artha-shastra* ("The Science of Material Gain"), a compilation of almost everything that had been written in India up to his time regarding *artha* (property, economics, or material success).

He was born into a Brahman family and received his education at Taxila (now in Pakistan). He is known to have had a knowledge of medicine and astrology, and it is believed he was familiar with elements of Greek and Persian learning introduced into India by Zoroastrians. Some authorities believe he was a Zoroastrian or at least was strongly influenced by that religion.

Kautilya became a counselor and adviser to Chandragupta

(reigned *c.* 321–*c.* 297), founder of the Mauryan empire of northern India, but lived by himself. He was instrumental in helping Chandragupta overthrow the powerful Nanda dynasty at Pataliputra, in the Magadha region.

Kautilya's book came to be Chandragupta's guide. Each of its 15 sections deals with a phase of government, which Kautilya sums up as "the science of punishment." He openly advises the development of an elaborate spy system reaching into all levels of society and encourages political and secret assassination. Lost for centuries, the book was discovered in 1905.

Compared by many to Italian statesman and writer Niccolò Machiavelli and by others to Aristotle and Plato, Kautilya is alternately condemned for his ruthlessness and trickery and praised for his sound political wisdom and knowledge of human nature. All authorities agree, however, that it was mainly because of Kautilya that the Mauryan empire under Chandragupta and later under Ashoka (reigned *c.* 265–*c.* 238) became a model of efficient government.

IBN KHALDUN

(May 27, 1332– March 17, 1406)

Ibn Khaldun is considered the greatest Arab historian. He was born in Tunis in 1332. At age 20, he was given a post at the court of Tunis, and served in politics, though with some controversy. He was suspected of participating in a rebellion and imprisoned. He once again returned to service, even being sent to conclude a peace treaty with Pedro I of Castille, but yet again, controversy followed him and he returned to Africa. During the next 10-year period Ibn Khaldun served as prime minister and in several other administrative capacities, led a punitive expedition, was robbed and stripped by nomads, and spent some time "studying and teaching."

A monument of Arab historian Ibn Khaldun.

In 1375, craving solitude from the exhausting business of politics, Ibn Khaldun took the most momentous step of his life: he sought refuge with the tribe of Awlad 'Arif, who lodged him and his family in the safety of a castle, Qal'at ibn Salamah, near what is now the town of Frenda, Algeria. There he spent four years, "free from all preoccupations," and wrote his massive masterpiece, the *Muqaddimah*, an introduction to history. It is difficult to overstress Ibn Khaldun's amazing originality. Muhsin Mahdi, a contemporary Iraqi-American scholar, has shown how much his approach and fundamental concepts owe to classical Islamic theology and philosophy, especially Averroism. And, of course, he drew liberally on the historical information accumulated by his predecessors and was doubtless influenced by their judgments. But nothing in these sources or, indeed, in any known Greek or Latin author can explain his deep insight into social phenomena, his firm grasp of the links binding the innumerable and apparently unrelated events that constitute the process of historical and social change.

NICCOLÒ MACHIAVELLI

(May 3, 1469–June 21, 1527)

Machiavelli was an Italian Renaissance political philosopher and states-man, secretary of the Florentine republic, whose most famous work, *The Prince (Il Principe)*, brought him a reputation as an atheist and an im-moral cynic. Machiavelli's family was wealthy and prominent, holding on occasion Florence's most important offices. His father, Bernardo, a doctor of laws, was nevertheless among the family's poorest members. At the age of 29, Machiavelli became head of the second chancery (*cancel-leria*), a post that placed him in charge of the republic's foreign affairs in subject territories.

During his tenure at the second chancery, Machiavelli persuaded Florence's chief magistrate to reduce the city's reliance on mercenary forces by establishing a militia (1505), which Machiavelli subsequently organized. He also undertook diplomatic and military missions to the court of France; to Cesare Borgia (1475/76–1507), the son of Pope Alexander VI (reigned 1492–1503); to Pope Julius II (reigned 1503–13), Alexander's successor; to the court of Holy Roman Emperor Maximilian I (reigned 1493–1519); and to Pisa (1509 and 1511).

In 1512 the Florentine republic was overthrown and the gonfalonier deposed by a Spanish army that Julius II had enlisted into his Holy League. The Medici family returned to rule Florence, and Machiavelli, suspected of conspiracy, was imprisoned, tortured, and sent into exile in 1513 to his father's small property in San Casciano, just south of Florence. There he wrote his two major works, *The Prince* and *Discourses on Livy*, both of which were published after his death. The former is ostensibly a book of advice to princes regarding the best means of acquiring and maintaining political power. For centuries it was regarded as dangerously wicked.

THOMAS HOBBES

(April 5, 1588–December 4, 1679)

Hobbes was an English philosopher, scientist, and historian, best known for his political philosophy, especially as articulated in his masterpiece *Leviathan* (1651). Hobbes viewed government primarily as a device for ensuring collective security. Political authority is justified by a hypothetical social contract among the many that vests in a sovereign person or entity the responsibility for the safety and well-being of all. In metaphysics, Hobbes defended materialism, the view that only material things are real. His scientific writings present all observed phenomena as the effects of matter in motion. Hobbes was not only a scientist in his own right but a great systematizer of the scientific findings of his contemporaries, including Galileo and Johannes Kepler. His enduring contribution is as a political philosopher who justified wide-ranging government powers on the basis of the self-interested consent of citizens.

Hobbes's political views exerted a discernible influence on his work in other fields, including historiography and legal theory. His political philosophy is chiefly concerned with the way in which government must be organized in order to avoid civil war. It therefore encompasses a view of the typical causes of civil war, all of which are represented in *Behemoth; or, The Long Parliament* (1679), his history of the English Civil Wars. Hobbes produced the first English translation of Thucydides' *History of the Peloponnesian War*, which he thought contained important lessons for his contemporaries regarding the excesses of democracy, the worst kind of dilution of sovereign authority, in his view.

For nearly the whole of his adult life, Hobbes worked for different branches of the wealthy and aristocratic Cavendish family. He served the family and their associates as translator, traveling companion, keeper of accounts, business representative, political adviser, and scientific collaborator.

Thomas Hobbes, English philosopher, scientist, and historian, best known for his political philosophy.

JOHN LOCKE

(August 29, 1632–October 28, 1704)

Locke was an English philosopher whose works lie at the foundation of modern philosophical empiricism and political liberalism. He was an inspirer of both the European Enlightenment and the Constitution of the United States. His philosophical thinking was close to that of the founders of modern science, especially Robert Boyle, Sir Isaac Newton, and other members of the Royal Society. His political thought was grounded in the notion of a social contract between citizens and in the importance of toleration, especially in matters of religion. Much of what he advocated in the realm of politics was accepted in England after the Glorious Revolution of 1688–89 and in the United States after the country's declaration of independence in 1776.

Locke's family was sympathetic to Puritanism but remained within the Church of England, a situation that coloured Locke's later life and thinking. Raised in Pensford, near Bristol, Locke was 10 years old at the start of the English Civil Wars between the monarchy of Charles I and parliamentary forces under the eventual leadership of Oliver Cromwell. After the first Civil War ended in 1646, Locke attended Westminster School in London. The curriculum of Westminster centred on Latin, Greek, Hebrew, Arabic, mathematics, and geography. In 1650 Locke was elected a King's Scholar, an academic honour. Locke's philosophies led him to a dual career as a physician and philosopher. He became a fellow of the Royal Society where he conducted scientific research. His most important philosophical work, *An Essay Concerning Human Understanding* (1689) began at a meeting with friends, probably in 1671.

Locke's political philosophy was guided by his deeply held religious commitments. Throughout his life he accepted the existence of a creating God and the notion that all humans are God's servants in virtue of that relationship. The essentially Protestant Christian framework of Locke's philosophy meant that his attitude toward Roman Catholicism would always be hostile. He rejected the claim of papal infallibility (how could it ever be proved?), and he feared the political dimensions of Catholicism as a threat to English autonomy, especially after Louis XIV in 1685 revoked the Edict of Nantes, which had granted religious liberty to the Protestant Huguenots.

JEAN-JACQUES ROUSSEAU
(June 28, 1717–July 2, 1778)

Rosseau was a Swiss-born philosopher, writer, and political theorist whose treatises and novels inspired the leaders of the French Revolution and the Romantic generation. Rousseau was the least academic of modern philosophers and in many ways was the most influential. His thought marked the end of the Age of Reason. He propelled political and ethical thinking into new channels. His reforms revolutionized taste, first in music, then in the other arts. He had a profound impact on people's way of life; he taught parents to take a new interest in their children and to educate them differently; he furthered the expression of emotion rather than polite restraint in friendship and love. He introduced the cult of religious sentiment among people who had discarded religious dogma. He opened people's eyes to the beauties of nature, and he made liberty an object of almost universal aspiration.

Rousseau was brought up by his father, who taught him to believe that the city of his birth was a republic as splendid as Sparta or ancient Rome. However, when he arrived in Paris at age 30, he joined a group of intellectuals gathered round the great French *Encyclopédie*, an organ of radical and anticlerical opinion. As part of what Rousseau called his "reform," or improvement of his own character, he began to look back at some of the austere principles that he had learned as a child in the Calvinist republic of Geneva. By the time his *Lettre à d'Alembert sur les spectacles (1758; Letter to Monsieur d'Alembert on the Theatre)* appeared in

133

Jean-Jacques Rousseau, philosopher, writer, and political theorist.

print, Rousseau had already left Paris to pursue a life closer to nature near Montmorency.

In his *Discours sur l'origine de l'inegalité* (1755; *Discourse on the Origin of Inequality*), Rousseau suggests that original humans were not social beings but entirely solitary, and to that extent he agrees with Hobbes's account of the state of nature. But in contrast to the English pessimist's view that human life in such a condition must have been "poor, nasty, brutish, and short," Rousseau claims that original humans were healthy, happy, good, and free. Human vices, he argued, date from the time when societies were formed. Civil society, as Rousseau describes it, comes into being to serve two purposes: to provide peace for everyone and to ensure the right to property for anyone lucky enough to have possessions. It is thus mostly to the advantage of the rich, since it transforms their de facto ownership into rightful ownership and keeps the poor dispossessed. Rousseau's *Du Contrat social* (1762; *The Social Contract*) begins with the sensational opening sentence: "Man is born free, and everywhere he is in chains," and proceeds to argue that men need not be in chains. If a civil society could be based on a genuine social contract, as opposed to the fraudulent social contract depicted in the *Discourse*, people would receive in exchange for their independence a better kind of freedom, namely true political, or republican, liberty.

MONTESQUIEU

(January 18, 1689–February 10, 1755)

Charles-Louis de Secondat, baron de La Brède et de Montesquieu was a French political philosopher whose major work, *The Spirit of Laws*, was a major contribution to political theory. His father, Jacques de Secondat, belonged to an old military family of modest wealth. When his mother died in 1696, the barony of La Brède passed to Charles-Louis, then aged seven. Educated first at home and then in the village, he was sent away to school in 1700, then continued his studies at the faculty of law at the University of Bordeaux. Soon thereafter, he married a wealthy woman and became financially and socially secure at the age of 27.

In 1721 he surprised all but a few close friends by publishing his *Lettres persanes (Persian Letters*, 1722), in which he gave a brilliant satirical portrait of French and particularly Parisian civilization, supposedly seen through the eyes of two Persian travellers. It pokes fun at all social classes and discusses, in its allegorical story of the Troglodytes, the theories of Thomas Hobbes relating to the state of nature. It also makes an original, if naive, contribution to the new science of demography, among other things. The success of this book launched his political career and he took a seat at the Académie Française in 1728. He later began to take more interest in literature, publishing several political works, beginning with *Considérations sur les causes de la grandeur des Romains et de leur décadence* (1734; *Reflections on the Causes of the Grandeur and Declension of the Romans*, 1734). After the publication of the *Considérations*, he rested for a short time and then, undismayed by failing eyesight, applied himself to this new and immense task. He undertook an extensive program of reading in law, history, economics, geography, and political theory, filling with his notes a large number of volumes, of which only one survives, *Geographica, tome II*. Subsequent works were *De l'esprit des loix; ou, du rapport que les loix doivent avoir avec la constitution de chaque gouvernement, les moeurs, le climat, la religion, le commerce, etc.*

135

(The Spirit of Laws, 1750), one of the great works in the history of political theory and in the history of jurisprudence, and his final work, *Essai sur le goût (Essay on Taste)*, with many between them.

ADAM SMITH

(c. June 5, 1723–July 17, 1790)

Smith was a Scottish social philosopher and political economist. He was the son by second marriage of Adam Smith, comptroller of customs at Kirkcaldy, a small (population 1,500) but thriving fishing village near Edinburgh, and Margaret Douglas, daughter of a substantial landowner. As an adult, owing to his mother's connections, Smith was able to give a series of public lectures in Edinburgh—a form of education then much in vogue in the prevailing spirit of "improvement." The lectures, which ranged over a wide variety of subjects from rhetoric to history and economics, made a deep impression on some of Smith's notable contemporaries. In 1751, at the age of 27, he was appointed professor of logic at Glasgow, from which post he transferred in 1752 to the more remunerative professorship of moral philosophy.

In 1759 Smith published his first work, *The Theory of Moral Sentiments*. Didactic, exhortative, and analytic by turns, it lays the psychological foundation on which *The Wealth of Nations* was later to be built. In it Smith described the principles of "human nature," which, together with Hume and the other leading philosophers of his time, he took as a universal and unchanging datum from which social institutions, as well as social behaviour, could be deduced. His second work, *The Wealth of Nations* is in fact a continuation of the philosophical theme begun in *The Theory of Moral Sentiments*. The ultimate problem to which Smith addresses himself is how the inner struggle between the passions and the "impartial spectator"—explicated in *Moral Sentiments* in terms of the single individual—works its effects in the larger arena of history itself, both in the long-run evolution of society and in terms of the immediate characteristics of the stage of history typical of Smith's own day.

EDMUND BURKE

(January 12, 1729–July 9, 1797)

Burke was a British statesman, parliamentary orator, and political thinker prominent in public life from 1765 to about 1795 and important in the history of political theory. He championed conservatism in opposition to Jacobinism in *Reflections on the Revolution in France* (1790).

Burke, the son of a solicitor, entered Trinity College, Dublin, in 1744 and moved to London in 1750 to begin his studies at the Middle Temple. After an unsuccessful first venture into politics, Burke was appointed secretary in 1765 to the Marquess of Rockingham, leader of one of the Whig groups, the largely liberal faction in Parliament, and he entered the House of Commons that year. Burke soon took an active part in the domestic constitutional controversy of George III's reign. The main problem during the 18th century was whether king or Parliament controlled the executive. Burke's chief comment on this issue is his pamphlet "Thoughts on the Cause of the Present Discontents" (1770). He argued that George's actions were against not the letter but the spirit of the constitution. In 1774 Burke was elected a member of Parliament for Bristol, then the second city of the kingdom and an open constituency requiring a genuine election contest. He held this seat for six years but failed to retain the confidence of his constituents.

A second great issue that confronted Burke in 1765 was the quarrel with the American colonies. Britain's imposition of the Stamp Act there in 1765, along with other measures, provoked unrest and opposition, which soon swelled into disobedience, conflict, and secession. Burke's best-known statements on this issue are two parliamentary speeches,

"On American Taxation" (1774) and "On Moving His Resolutions for Conciliation with the Colonies" (1775), and "A Letter to…the Sheriffs of Bristol, on the Affairs of America" (1777). British policy, he argued, had been both imprudent and inconsistent, but above all legalistic and intransigent, in the assertion of imperial rights. Authority must be exercised with respect for the temper of those subject to it, if there was not to be collision of power and opinion. This truth was being ignored in the imperial quarrel; it was absurd to treat universal disobedience as criminal: the revolt of a whole people argued serious misgovernment.

Burke also tried to address the issue of Irish independence, and the issue of Indian independence, which he considered to be the larger task. Burke concluded that the corrupt state of Indian government under British rule could be remedied only if the vast patronage it was bound to dispose of was in the hands neither of a company nor of the crown.

HENRI DE SAINT-SIMON

(October 17, 1760–May 19, 1825)

Saint-Simon was a French social theorist and one of the chief founders of Christian socialism. Saint-Simon was born of an impoverished aristocratic family. He entered military service at 17, and was sent to aid the American colonies in their war against England. He remained in France during the French Revolution, bought lands, but was imprisoned in the Palais de Luxembourg, but when he emerged, he was very wealthy. Unfortunately he was unable to hold on to his gains and turned to the study of science. His first published work, *Lettres d'un habitant de Genève à ses contemporains* (1803; "Letters of an Inhabitant of Geneva to His Contemporaries"), Saint-Simon proposed that scientists take the place of priests in the social order. He argued that the property owners who held political power could hope to maintain themselves against the propertyless only by subsidizing the advance of knowledge.

Throughout his life Saint-Simon devoted himself to a long series of projects and publications through which he sought to win support for his social ideas. As a thinker, Saint-Simon was deficient in system, clearness, and coherence, but his influence on modern thought, especially in the social sciences, is undeniable. Apart from the details of his socialist teachings, his main ideas are simple and represented a reaction against the bloodletting of the French Revolution and the militarism of Napoleon. Saint-Simon correctly foresaw the industrialization of the world, and he believed that science and technology would solve most of humanity's problems.

Saint-Simon died in 1825, and by 1826 a movement supporting his ideas had begun to grow. In July 1830 his disciples, the Saint-Simonians, issued a proclamation demanding the ownership of goods in common, the abolition of the right of inheritance, and the enfranchisement of women. Although the movement fragmented and broke up, the Saint-Simonians had a pervasive influence on the intellectual life of 19th-century Europe.

AUGUSTE COMTE

(January 19, 1798–September 5, 1857)

Comte was a French philosopher known as the founder of sociology and positivism. His father, Louis Comte, a tax official, and his mother, Rosalie Boyer, were strongly royalist and deeply sincere Roman Catholics. But their sympathies were at odds with the republicanism and skepticism that swept through France in the aftermath of the French Revolution. Comte resolved these conflicts at an early age by rejecting Roman Catholicism and royalism alike. Comte attended the École Polytechnique and read widely in philosophy and history and was especially interested in those thinkers who were beginning to discern and trace some order in the history of human society. He met Henri de Saint-Simon in Paris and found that their ideas were very similar, at least at first. In 1826 Comte began a series of lectures on his "system of positive philosophy" for a private audience. In 1828/29 he again took up his projected lecture series. This was so successfully concluded that he redelivered it at the Royal Athenaeum during 1829–30. The following 12 years were devoted to his publication (in six volumes) of his philosophy in a work entitled *Cours de philosophie positive* (1830–42; "Course of Positive Philosophy"; Eng. trans. *The Positive Philosophy of Auguste Comte*).

His other major work was the *Système de politique positive*, 4 vol. (1851–54; *System of Positive Polity*), in which he completed his formulation of sociology. The entire work emphasized morality and moral progress as the central preoccupation of human knowledge and effort and gave an account of the polity, or political organization, that this required. Comte lived to see his writings widely scrutinized throughout Europe. Many English intellectuals were influenced by him, and they translated and promulgated his work. His French devotees had also increased, and a large correspondence developed with positivist societies throughout the world. Comte died of cancer in 1857.

KARL MARX

(May 5, 1818–March 14, 1883)

Karl Heinrich Marx was a revolutionary, sociologist, historian, and economist. He published (with Friedrich Engels) *Manifest der Kommunistischen Partei* (1848), commonly known as *The Communist Manifesto,* the most celebrated pamphlet in the history of the socialist movement. He also was the author of the movement's most important book, *Das Kapital.*

Karl Heinrich Marx was the oldest surviving boy of nine children. Both his parents were Jewish but his father was baptized in the Evangelical Established Church a year before Marx's birth. Marx received a liberal education, attended the University of Bonn and took courses in humanities, then enrolled at the University of Berlin to study law and philosophy. In 1842, Marx began to contribute to a liberal newspaper and later became its editor. After Prussian authorities suspended the publication, Marx agreed to coedit with the liberal Hegelian Arnold Ruge a new review, the *Deutsch-französische Jahrbücher* ("German-French Yearbooks"), which was to be published in Paris. Though the yearbooks were short-lived, they led Marx to befriend Friedrich Engels, who became his lifelong collaborator.

An unusual sequence of events led Marx and Engels to write their pamphlet *The Communist Manifesto*. In June 1847 a secret society, the League of the Just, composed mainly of emigrant German handicraftsmen, met in London and decided to formulate a political program. They sent a representative to Marx to ask him to join the league; Marx overcame his doubts and, with Engels, joined the organization, which thereupon changed its name to the Communist League and enacted a democratic constitution. Entrusted with the task of composing their program, Marx and Engels worked from the middle of December 1847 to the end of January 1848. The London Communists were already impatiently threatening Marx with disciplinary action when he sent them the manuscript; they promptly adopted it as their manifesto.

In 1859 Marx published his first book on economic theory, *Zur Kritik der politischen Ökonomie (A Contribution to the Critique of Political Economy)*. In its preface he again summarized his materialistic conception of history, his theory that the course of history is dependent on economic developments. Economic fortune however, was not Marx's fate. He found himself in political isolation and financial ruin for years depending on handouts from Engel and his family. He had a brief resurgence during the 1870s, but after the death of his wife and eldest daughter, he died in London in 1883. His other great work, *Das Kapital* was published after his death.

Karl Marx worked with Friedrich Engels to publish *The Communist Manifesto.*

FRIEDRICH ENGELS

(November 28, 1820–August 5, 1895)

Engels was a German socialist philosopher, the closest collaborator of Karl Marx in the foundation of modern communism. They coauthored *The Communist Manifesto* (1848), and Engels edited the second and third volumes of *Das Kapital* after Marx's death. Engels grew up in a family with moderately liberal political views. Though interested in poetry, Engels father insisted that he work expanding the family business. He went to Bremen to work in business and also exhibited a talent for journalism. He then volunteered in an artillery regiment, learning military matters that became one of his specialties.

In 1842 he met Moses Hess who converted him to communism. He sometimes joined the group of philosophers Marx belonged to, and their friendship was established when the two went on a 10-day visit to Paris. Shortly after, Engels published *Die Lage der arbeitenden Klasse in England* (1845; *The Condition of the Working Class in England*). Their first major joint work was *Die deutsche Ideologie (1845; The German Ideology)*, which, however, was not published until more than 80 years later.

The revolutions of 1848, which were precipitated by the attempt of the German states to throw off an authoritarian, almost feudal, political system and replace it with a constitutional, representative form of government, was a momentous event in the lives of Marx and Engels. It was their only opportunity to participate directly in a revolution and to demonstrate their flexibility as revolutionary tacticians with the aim of turning the revolution into a communist victory. Their major tool was the newspaper *Neue Rheinische Zeitung,* which Marx edited in Cologne with the able assistance of Engels. After the failure of the revolution, Engels and Marx were reunited in London, where they reorganized the Communist League and drafted tactical directives for the communists in the belief that another revolution would soon take place. But how to replace his depleted income soon became Engels's main problem. He also found himself giving financial support to Marx.

After Marx's death (1883), Engels served as the foremost authority on Marx and Marxism. Aside from occasional writings on a variety of subjects and introductions to new editions of Marx's works, Engels completed volumes 2 and 3 of *Das Kapital* (1885 and 1894) on the basis of Marx's uncompleted manuscripts and rough notes. Engels's other two late publications were the books *Der Ursprung der Familie, des Privateigenthums und des Staats* (1884; *The Origin of the Family, Private Property and the State*) and *Ludwig Feuerbach und der Ausgang der klassischen deutschen Philosophie* (1888; *Ludwig Feuerbach and the Outcome of Classical German Philosophy*).

ARTHUR F. BENTLEY

(October 16, 1870–May 21, 1957)

Arthur Fisher Bentley was an American political scientist and philosopher known for his work in epistemology, logic, and linguistics and for his contributions to the development of a behavioral methodology of political science.

Bentley received a B.A. in 1892 and a Ph.D. in 1895 from Johns Hopkins University and taught a seminar in sociology the following year at the University of Chicago. He then engaged in reporting and editorial work for the *Times-Herald* and *Record-Herald* of Chicago until 1910, when he retired to Paoli, Ind., to manage his orchard and write. He was active in the Red Cross during World War I and was Indiana leader of the presidential campaign of Senator Robert M. La Follette of the Progressive Party in 1924.

In *The Process of Government: A Study of Social Pressures* (1908), his most noted work, Bentley attempted to develop a methodology of behavioral social-science research and urged concentration of study on overt human activity, the raw material of the political process. He arranged political data in terms of groups, interests, and pressures (a given activity might be viewed as the activity of a group, the expression of an interest, or the exertion of pressure). He did not attempt to formulate a general group theory and in his later work was prepared to consider the individual as the focal point of inquiry into the political process. Concerned more with methodology than with theory, he saw the study of manifest behaviour as the way to more profound understanding of human affairs. Together with the philosopher John Dewey, Bentley developed a "transactional" view of social explanation that went beyond the existing prescientific "self-action" and mechanistic "interaction" approaches and postulated knowledge as a social phenomenon.

In *The Process of Government* Bentley dealt with the social nature of language, in which all description and thought are to be found. Other works by Bentley include *Relativity in Man and Society* (1926), *Linguistic Analysis of Mathematics* (1932), *Behavior, Knowledge, Fact* (1935), *Knowing and the Known* (1949, with John Dewey), and *Inquiry into Inquiries: Essays in Social Theory* (1954).

HAROLD DWIGHT LASSWELL

(February 13, 1902–December 18, 1978)

Lasswell was an influential political scientist known for seminal studies of power relations and of personality and politics and for other major contributions to contemporary behavioral political science.

Lasswell received his bachelor's degree in philosophy and economics in 1922 and his Ph.D. in 1926 from the University of Chicago, and he studied at the Universities of London, Geneva, Paris, and Berlin during several summers in the 1920s. He taught political science at the University of Chicago (1922–38) and then served at the Washington

School of Psychiatry (1938–39) and was director of war communications research at the U.S. Library of Congress (1939–45). After World War II, he went to Yale University, where he served in various capacities He was also a professor of law at John Jay College of the City University of New York and at Temple University. He was a visiting lecturer at campuses throughout the world and was a consultant to numerous U.S. government agencies.

Lasswell viewed political science as the study of changes in the distribution of value patterns in society, and, because distribution depends on power, the focal point of his analysis was power dynamics. He defined values as desired goals and power as the ability to participate in decisions, and he conceived political power as the ability to produce intended effects on other people. In *Politics: Who Gets What, When, How* (1936)—a work whose title later served as the standard lay definition of politics—he viewed the elite as the primary holders of power, but in *Power and Society: A Framework for Political Inquiry* (1950), written with Abraham Kaplan, the discussion was broadened to include a general framework for political inquiry that examined key analytic categories such as person, personality, group, and culture.

His works on political psychology include *Psychopathology and Politics* (1930), which seeks the means of channeling the desire for domination to healthy ends; *World Politics and Personal Insecurity* (1935); and *Power and Personality* (1948), which deals with the problem of power seekers who sublimate their personal frustrations in power. In these and later works, Lasswell moved toward a moralistic posture, calling for the social and biological sciences to reorient themselves toward a science of social policy that would serve the democratic will for justice. Other features of political science that can be traced to Lasswell include systems theory, functional and role analysis, and content analysis.

Some of his other major works include *Propaganda Technique in the World War* (1927), *World Revolutionary Propaganda* (with Dorothy Blumenstock, 1939), *Politics Faces Economics* (1946), *The Policy Sciences: Recent Developments in Scope and Method* (with Daniel Lerner, 1951), and *The Future of Political Science* (1963).

V.O. KEY, JR.

(March 13, 1908–October 4, 1963)

Key was a U.S. political scientist known for his studies of the U.S. political process and for his contributions to the development of a more empirical and behavioral political science.

Educated at the University of Texas (B.A., 1929; M.A., 1930) and the University of Chicago (Ph.D., 1934), Key joined the faculty of the University of California at Los Angeles. In 1936–38 he served with the Social Science Research Council and the National Resources Planning Board. He taught at Johns Hopkins University (1938–49) with interruptions for government service with the Bureau of the Budget during World War II. He taught at Yale in 1949–51 and at Harvard University from 1951 until his death.

In 1942 Key published *Politics, Parties, and Pressure Groups,* in which he analyzed the part played by organized interests in the political process. His *Southern Politics in State and Nation* (1949) pioneered the use of quantitative techniques and was a classic in regional political studies. In *Public Opinion and American Democracy* (1961) he analyzed the link between the changing patterns of public opinion and the governmental system. He was vigorous in opposing the idea that voters' preferences are socially determined, and in his posthumous work, *The Responsible Electorate: Rationality in Presidential Voting 1936–60* (1966), he analyzed public opinion data and electoral returns to show what he believed to be the rationality of voters' choices. Other works by Key include *The Techniques of Political Graft in the United States* (1936), *A Primer of Statistics for Political Scientists* (1954), and *American State Politics: An Introduction* (1956). He served as president of the American Political Science Association in 1958–59.

WILLIAM RIKER

(September 22, 1920–June 26, 1993)

William Harrison Riker was an American political scientist who popularized the use of mathematical models, and in particular game theory, in the study of political behaviour.

Riker graduated from Shortridge High School in Indianapolis in 1938 and attended DePauw University in Greencastle (B.A., 1942). Because of his country's involvement in World War II, Riker decided to defer his graduate studies and joined the Radio Corporation of America (later RCA Corporation). He resumed his studies after the war, receiving a Ph.D. in government from Harvard University in 1948. As a professor and department chair at the University of Rochester, Riker transformed the political science department into a flagship of positive political theory, a term he coined to describe his approach, which aimed to produce empirically verifiable theories of political behaviour. Riker and his department were so closely connected that Riker's approach came to be known as the Rochester School of Political Science.

Riker introduced the use of formal modeling. Riker labeled his theory "positive political theory," because it endeavoured to produce only statements that are falsifiable and can be empirically verified. Riker's scientific model of political behaviour is also known as a form of public choice theory, or rational choice theory, because it relies on the assumption that individuals base their decisions on their calculation of costs and benefits and their desire to maximize the latter.

Riker also exercised a profound and lasting influence on the study of federalism. In his *Federalism: Origin, Operation, Significance* (1964), he rejected the idea that federalism in the United States originated in the desire of the founders to promote a common good or to defend liberty against the encroachment of central government. Riker defined federalism as a form of political organization in which different levels

148

of government (regional, central) have authority over different issue areas. Riker also emphasized the importance of the party system. The more the central parties control the parties competing at the state or regional level, he believed, the more centralized the federal system will be.

Riker's other seminal publications include *The Theory of Political Coalitions* (1962) and *Liberalism Against Populism* (1982). He served as president of the Public Choice Society (1966), a group dedicated to the advancement of public choice theory across disciplinary lines, and of the American Political Science Association (1982–83). Riker was also one of the first political scientists to be elected a member of the National Academy of Sciences.

American political scientist William Riker.

ROBERT A. DAHL

(December 17, 1915–February 5, 2014)

Robert Alan Dahl was an American political scientist and educator. A leading theorist of political pluralism, Dahl stressed the role in politics played by associations, groups, and organizations.

Dahl was a graduate of the University of Washington (A.B., 1936) and obtained a Ph.D. from Yale University in 1940. He served in the U.S. Army during World War II and was awarded the Bronze Star (with cluster) for distinguished service. After the war, Dahl returned to Yale, where he taught until 1986. He subsequently became Sterling Professor Emeritus of Political Science and Senior Research Scientist Sociology.

In *The Concept of Power* (1957), his first major contribution to the field of political science, Dahl developed an operational definition of power: "A has power over B to the extent that he can get B to do something that B would not otherwise do." Dahl argued that his definition could be used to compare the power of political actors in a given sphere—for instance, the influence of different U.S. senators on questions of foreign policy.

In his best-known work, *Who Governs?: Democracy and Power in an American City* (1961), a study of power dynamics in New Haven, Conn., Dahl argued that political power in the United States is pluralistic. He introduced the term *polyarchy* to characterize American politics and other political systems that are open, inclusive, and competitive (*Polyarchy*, 1971). Polyarchies are based on the principle of representative rather than direct democracy and therefore constitute a form of minority rule, yet they are also (imperfectly) democratized systems that limit the power of elite groups through institutions such as regular and free elections.

Despite his critique of elite-power theory, Dahl was faulted after the publication of *Who Governs?* for underestimating the importance of broad-based civic participation. Later, in *Democracy and Its Critics* (1989), he recognized the value of an active citizenry and associated polyarchy with political rights such as freedom of expression and association.

Dahl's other works include *A Preface to Democratic Theory* (1956); *After the Revolution?: Authority in a Good Society* (1970); *Size and Democracy* (1973), coauthored with Edward R. Tufte; *A Preface to Economic Democracy* (1985); *On Democracy* (1998); and *How Democratic Is the American Constitution?* (2001). He served as president of the

American Political Science Association (1966–67) and was a member of numerous research organizations and learned societies, including the National Academy of Sciences, the American Philosophical Society, the American Academy of Arts and Sciences, and the British Academy.

CONCLUSION

Changes in culture, whether slowly over decades or quickly due to a forcible shift such as world war, and changes in technology or the environment have forced political systems to be dynamic. Fundamental theories and ideas have changed with the needs and desires of cultures, as power has crumbled as it did at the end of the Russian Revolution, been slowly built as it was during the heyday of the Roman empire, or hastily seized as in the aftermath of war. Political philosophies have made great changes since the early days of Plato, yet these early philosophies provide the foundation, framework, and lexicon used to build on and discuss politics today.

A study of the great civilizations that ushered in the birth of political science and political philosophy is essential to understanding how modern political systems work and why they must be flexible in order to meet the demands of an ever-changing society. It is also essential to the understanding that politics can and should be changed by the will of the people.

ABSOLUTISM The political doctrine and practice of unlimited, centralized authority and absolute sovereignty, as vested especially in a monarch or dictator.

APPORTIONMENT An act or result of dividing something among or between people.

AUTHORITARIANISM The principle of blind submission to authority, as opposed to individual freedom of thought and action.

BEHAVIORALISM The view that the subject matter of political sciece should be limited to phenomena that are independently observable and quantifiable.

BOND A loan contract issued by a government or corporation specifying an obligation to return borrowed funds with interest.

BOURGEOISIE The middle class.

BUREAUCRACY A group of unelected people involved in running a government. A system of government that operates under a complicated set of rules.

CONSTITUENCIES Groups who support a particular politician or political party. Voting districts.

DESPOTISM A system of rule by a person who has total power and who often uses that power in cruel and unfair ways.

DICTATORSHIP Rule or control by one person with total power.

ENFEOFFED Invested with a fief, a large area of land ruled over by a lord.

FEDERALIST A supporter of federal government, especially a supporter of the U.S. Constitution.

OLIGARCHY Government or control by a small group of people.

PARTISAN A firm adherent of a political party, faction, cause, or person, especially one exhibiting blind, prejudiced, and unreasoning allegiance.

PLEBISCITES Votes by which the people of a country or region express their opinion for or against an important proposal.

PLURALIST One who believes that people of different social classes, religions, or races should live together in a society.

PROLETARIAT The labouring class, especially the class of industrial workers who lack their own means of production and hence sell their labour to live.

REFERENDUM An event in which the people of a county or state vote for or against a law that deals with a specific issue. A public vote on a particular issue.

REGIME A form of government.

SOCIALISM A way of organizing a society in which major industries are owned and controlled by the public rather than by individual people and companies.

SOCIOLOGY The study of society, social institutions, and social relationships.

STATISM The concentration of economic controls and planning in the hands of a highly centralized government, often extending to government ownership of industry.

TYRANNY A government in which all power belongs to one person.

CONSTITUTION

Current texts of more than 150 national constitutions are available in English translation in Albert P. Blaustein and Gisbert H. Flanz (eds.), *Constitutions of the Countries of the World*, 20 vol. (1971–), issued in looseleaf format and updated frequently. Another compendium of constitutions is Amos J. Peaslee, *Constitutions of Nations*, rev. 3rd ed. by Dorothy Peaslee Xydis, 4 vol. in 7 (1965–70), and a rev. 4th ed. of vol. 1–2 (1974–85). Famous constitutions, at the national as well as subnational levels, are collected in Albert P. Blaustein and Jay A. Sigler (eds.), *Constitutions That Made History* (1988). John J. Wuest and Manfred C. Vernon (eds.), *New Source Book in Major European Governments* (1966), provides excerpts of constitutional documents of the major governments in Europe.

An intellectual overview is provided by A.V. Dicey, *Introduction to the Study of the Law of the Constitution*, 10th ed. (1959, reissued 1985). Aristotle's classic work on politics is available as *The Politics of Aristotle*, trans. and ed. by Ernest Barker (1946, reissued 1972); while more recent classic works are collected in Ernest Barker (ed.), *Social Contract: Essays by Locke, Hume, and Rousseau* (1947, reissued 1980). Robert R. Bowie and Carl J. Friedrich (eds.), *Studies in Federalism* (1954), is another important source. William S. Livingston, *Federalism and Constitutional Change* (1956, reprinted 1974), stands as the best study of constitutional change. Herbert J. Spiro, *Government by Constitution: The Political Systems of Democracy* (1959), is a valuable study, while his *Responsibility in Government: Theory and Practice* (1969) focuses on the related problems of accountability and responsibility. Carl J. Friedrich, *Constitutional Government and Democracy: Theory and Practice in Europe and America*, 4th ed. (1968), is a comprehensive treatment. Additional important works include Ivor Jennings, *Cabinet Government*, 3rd ed. (1969); Edward McWhinney, *Judicial Review*, 4th ed. (1969), and *Constitution-Making: Principles, Process, Practice* (1981); and Jon Elster and Rune Slagstad (eds.), *Constitutionalism and Democracy* (1988).

Walter Bagehot, *The English Constitution* (1867, reissued 1993), remains a classic exposition. The best history of the origins of English constitutionalism is Charles Howard McIlwain, *The High Court of Parliament and Its Supremacy: An Historical Essay on the Boundaries Between Legislation and Adjudication in England* (1910, reprinted 1979). Francis Dunham Wormuth, *The Origins of Modern Constitutionalism* (1949), is another useful work.

Alexander Hamilton, James Madison, and John Jay, *The Federalist* (1788), has been reissued many times and is indispensable for understanding the origins of American constitutionalism. The basis of American constitutionalism is ably traced in Donald S. Lutz, *The Origins of American Constitutionalism* (1988); and David A.J. Richards, *Foundations of American Constitutionalism* (1989). Discussions of the impact of the American constitution upon the political process include Sarah Baumgartner Thurow (ed.), *Constitutionalism in America,* vol. 3, *Constitutionalism in Perspective: The United States Constitution in Twentieth Century Politics* (1988); and *Corwin & Peltason's Understanding the Constitution,* 13th ed. by J.W. Peltason (1991).

Samuel H. Beer and Adam B. Ulam (eds.), *Patterns of Government: The Major Political Systems of Europe,* 3rd ed. (1973), provides a useful analysis. Studies of French constitutionalism include Stanley Hoffmann et al., *In Search of France* (1963), and *Decline or Renewal?: France Since the 1930s* (1974). Ralf Dahrendorf, *Society and Democracy in Germany* (1967, reprinted 1992; originally published in German, 1965), is a sociological account; it is complemented by Arnold J. Heidenheimer and Donald P. Kommers, *The Governments of Germany,* 4th ed. (1975). The concept of congruence between political and social patterns of authority is examined in Harry Eckstein, *Division and Cohesion in Democracy: A Study of Norway* (1966). Constitutionalism in the European Community is discussed in Vernon Bogdanor (ed.), *Constitutions in Democratic Politics* (1988), on the European Community. The impact of American constitutionalism upon other nations is the topic of George Athan Billias (ed.), *American Constitutionalism Abroad: Selected Essays in Comparative*

Constitutional History (1990).

Studies of constitutional development include Herbert J. Spiro (ed.), *Patterns of African Development: Five Comparisons* (1967); B.O. Nwabueze, *Constitutionalism in the Emergent States* (1973); Lawrence Ward Beer (ed.), *Constitutionalism in Asia: Asian Views of the American Influence* (1979); and William B. Simons (ed.), *The Constitutions of the Communist World* (1980), still of historical interest. The potential role of constitutions in resolving societal conflict is considered in Albert P. Blaustein and Dana Blaustein Epstein, *Resolving Language Conflicts: A Study of the World's Constitutions* (1986). Douglas Greenberg et al. (eds.), *Constitutionalism and Democracy: Transitions in the Contemporary World: The American Council of Learned Societies Comparative Constitutionalism Papers* (1993), offers an excellent compilation of studies of constitutionalism after the recent transitions to democracy.

ELECTION

A classic English-language review of the history of elections is Charles Seymour and Donald Paige Frary, *How the World Votes: The Story of Democratic Development in Elections*, 2 vol. (1918). A readable, comprehensive overview of electoral institutions is David M. Farrell, *Electoral Systems: A Comparative Introduction* (2001). The impact of electoral systems on party systems is analyzed in Douglas W. Rae, *The Political Consequences of Electoral Laws*, rev. ed. (1971); Rein Taagepera and Matthew Soberg Shugart, *Seats and Votes: The Effects and Determinants of Electoral Systems* (1989, reissued 1991); and Arend Lijphart et al., *Electoral Systems and Party Systems: A Study of Twenty-seven Democracies, 1945–1990* (1994). The significance for democratic theory of electoral arrangements is considered in Richard S. Katz, *Democracy and Elections* (1997). The development of mixed-member electoral systems is the focus of Matthew Soberg Shugart and Martin P. Wattenberg (eds.), *Mixed-Member Electoral Systems: The Best of Both Worlds?* (2001).

Analyses of referenda and direct democracy can be found in David B. Magleby, *Direct Legislation: Voting on Ballot Propositions in the United States* (1984); Thomas E. Cronin, *Direct Democracy: The Politics of Initiative, Referendum, and Recall* (1989, reissued 1999); David Butler and Austin Ranney (eds.), *Referendums Around the World: The Growing Use of Direct Democracy* (1994); and Ian Budge, *The New Challenge of Direct Democracy* (1996).

Classic perspectives on voting behaviour and electoral participation can be found in Anthony Downs, *An Economic Theory of Democracy* (1957, reissued 1965); Angus Campbell et al., *The American Voter* (1960, reprinted 1980); and Seymour M. Lipset and Stein Rokkan (eds.), *Party Systems and Voter Alignments: Cross-National Perspectives* (1967). Other developments in voting behaviour are discussed in Ivor Crewe and David Denver (eds.), *Electoral Change in Western Democracies: Patterns and Sources of Electoral Volatility* (1985); Stefano Bartolini and Peter Mair, *Identity, Competition and Electoral Availability: The Stabilisation of European Electorates, 1885–1985* (1990); Mark N. Franklin et al., *Electoral Change: Responses to Evolving Social and Attitudinal Structures in Western Countries* (1992); Samuel L. Popkin, *The Reasoning Voter: Communication and Persuasion in Presidential Campaigns*, 2nd ed. (1994); Warren E. Miller and J. Merrill Shanks, *The New American Voter* (1996); Geoffrey Evans (ed.), *The End of Class Politics?: Class Voting in Comparative Context* (1999); and Samuel Merrill III and Bernard Grofman, *A Unified Theory of Voting: Directional and Proximity Spatial Models* (1999).

LIBERALISM

The foundations of liberalism were laid in Thomas Hobbes, *Leviathan* (1651); and John Locke, *Two Treatises of Government* (1690), especially the second treatise. Other important contributions are Adam Smith, *An Inquiry into the Nature and Causes of the Wealth of Nations* (1776); Alexander Hamilton, James Madison, and John Jay, *The Federalist* (1788); Jeremy Bentham, *An Introduction to the Principles of Morals and Legislation* (1789); James Mill, *An Essay on Government* (1820, reissued 1955); Alexis de Tocqueville, *De la démocratie en Amérique* (1835; *Democracy in America*, 1835); John Stuart Mill, *On Liberty* (1859), *Considerations on Representative Government* (1861, reprinted 1991), and *The Subjection of Women* (1869, reissued 1997); and Thomas Hill Green, "Lectures on the Principles of Political Obligation," in R.L. Nettleship (ed.), *Works of Thomas Hill Green*, vol. 2, *Philosophical Works* (1886, reprinted 1997; also reissued separately as *Lectures on the Principles of Political Obligation and Other Writings*, ed. by Paul Harris and John Morrow, 1986).

Classic works of the 20th century include L.T. Hobhouse, *Liberalism* (1911); John Maynard Keynes, *The General Theory of Employment, Interest, and Money* (1936); and F.A. Hayek, *The Road to Serfdom* (1944), and *The Constitution of Liberty* (1960).

General studies of liberalism include Guido de Ruggiero, *The History of European Liberalism* (1927, reprinted 1981; originally published in Italian, 1925); Robert Denoon Cumming, *Human Nature and History: A Study of the Development of Liberal Political Thought* (1969); Louis Hartz, *The Liberal Tradition in America: An Interpretation of American Political Thought Since the Revolution* (1955, reprinted 1991); Kenneth R. Minogue, *The Liberal Mind* (1963, reissued 2000); Eldon J. Eisenach, *Two Worlds of Liberalism: Religion and Politics in Hobbes, Locke, and Mill* (1981); Thomas A. Spragens, Jr., *The Irony of Liberal Reason* (1981); Knud Haakonssen (ed.), *Traditions of Liberalism* (1988); John Gray, *Beyond the New Right: Markets, Government, and the Common Environment* (1993), and *The Two Faces of Liberalism* (2000); and Charles K. Rowley (ed.), *The Political Economy of the Minimal State* (1996).

The most influential works in contemporary liberal political philosophy are John Rawls, *A Theory of Justice*, rev. ed. (1999), and *Political Liberalism*, expanded ed. (2005), supplemented by *Justice as Fairness: A Restatement*, ed. by Erin Kelly (2001); and Robert Nozick, *Anarchy, State, and Utopia* (1974, reissued 2003). Accounts of liberalism as a doctrine that is neutral with regard to conceptions of the good include Bruce A. Ackerman, *Social Justice in the Liberal State* (1980); Ronald Dworkin, *Taking Rights Seriously* (1977); and Charles E. Larmore, *Patterns of Moral Complexity* (1987). Criticism of this view is offered in Joseph Raz, *The Morality of Freedom* (1986); William A. Galston, *Liberal Purposes: Goods, Virtues, and Diversity in the Liberal State* (1991); and Michael J. Sandel, *Liberalism and the Limits of Justice*, 2nd ed. (1998). Susan Moller Okin, *Justice, Gender, and the Family* (1989), is a clear statement of liberal feminism.

POLITICAL PHILOSOPHY

George Holland Sabine, *A History of Political Theory*, 4th ed., rev. by Thomas Landon Thorson (1973), provides a comprehensive survey. William Archibald Dunning, *A History of Political Theories*, 3 vol. (1902–20, reissued 1936–38), is still valuable. Also of interest is K.R. Popper, *The Open Society and Its Enemies*, 5th ed., rev., 2 vol. (1966). Additional surveys that will be useful include Leo Strauss and Joseph Cropsey (eds.), *History of Political Philosophy*, 2nd ed. (1972, reprinted 1981); Leo Rauch, *The Political Animal: Studies in Political Philosophy from Machiavelli to Marx* (1981); and Anthony Pagden (ed.), *The Languages of Political Theory in Early-Modern Europe* (1987). Ernest Barker, *Principles of Social & Political Theory* (1951, reissued 1980), analyzes essential problems. Other important works are John Bowle, *Politics and Opinion in the Nineteenth Century* (1954, reissued 1966); William Ebenstein, *Modern Political Thought: The Great Issues*, 2nd ed. (1960); Harold D. Lasswell, *The Future of Political Science* (1962, reissued 1974); and Joseph Cropsey, *Political Philosophy and the Issues of Politics* (1977, reissued 1980).

POLITICAL SCIENCE

Works of classical political philosophy contain vast and valuable insights that influence current scholars whether they are aware of them or not. Aristotle's *Politics* and Machiavelli's *The Prince* must be counted as the discipline's founding classics. The intellectual basis for modern democracy can be found in John Locke, *Two Treatises on Civil Government* (1690). The foundation for studies of political culture is Alexis de Tocqueville, *Democracy in America* (1835–40). Weber's work is well summarized in H.H. Gerth and C. Wright Mills (eds.), *From Max Weber: Essays in Sociology* (1946, reprinted 1998); and in Reinhard Bendix, *Max Weber: An Intellectual Portrait* (1960, reissued 1998).

A critical overview of 20th-century developments is Karl W. Deutsch, Andrei S. Markovits, and John Platt (eds.), *Advances in the Social Sciences, 1900–1980: What, Who, Where, How* (1986). The view that political science has too closely aped the natural sciences is presented by David Ricci, *The Tragedy of Political Science: Politics, Scholarship, and Democracy* (1984, reissued 1987).

There are few modern classics, but among those considered indispensable are Joseph Schumpeter, *Capitalism, Socialism and Democracy*, 6th ed. (1987); E.E. Schattschneider, *The Semisovereign People: A Realist's View of Democracy in America* (1960, reissued 1988); and V.O. Key, *Politics, Parties and Pressure Groups*, 5th ed. (1964), and *The Responsible Electorate* (1966, reissued 1968). Modern political theory, including rational choice theory, owes much to Mancur Olson, *The Logic of Collective Action: Public Goods and the Theory of Groups* (1968, reissued 1995). Samuel P. Huntington has been a major force in post-World War II political science, especially his *Political Order in Changing Societies* (1968) and *The Clash of Civilizations and the Remaking of World Order* (1996). Robert A. Dahl, *Modern Political Analysis*, 5th ed. (1991), is an excellent guide to the renowned political scientist's views. Seymour Martin Lipset, *Political Man: The Social Bases of Politics* (1960), is a prime example of the behavioral approach, and his *American Exceptionalism: A*

Double-Edged Sword (1996) illustrates the historical-cultural approach. The historical-cultural perspective is also the focus of Robert Putnam, *Making Democracy Work: Civic Traditions in Modern Italy* (1993), and *Bowling Alone: The Collapse and Revival of American Community* (2001).

Introductory works on comparative politics include Ruth Lane, *The Art of Comparative Politics* (1996); Arend Lijphart, *Electoral Systems and Party Systems: A Study of Twenty-seven Democracies, 1945–1990* (1994); B. Guy Peters, *Comparative Politics: Theory and Method* (1998); Michael G. Roskin, *Countries and Concepts: Politics, Geography, and Culture*, 8th ed. (2004); and Alfred Stepan, *Arguing Comparative Politics* (2001).

An excellent overview of the field of international relations is James E. Dougherty and Robert L. Pfaltzgraff, Jr., *Contending Theories of International Relations*, 5th ed. (2001). A critical and philosophical overview is Raymond Aron, *Peace and War: A Theory of International Relations* (1973, reprinted 1981; originally published in French, 1962). The realist approach in international relations is presented in Hans J. Morgenthau, *Politics Among Nations: The Struggle for Power and Peace* (1948); and in Henry Kissinger, *Diplomacy* (1994).

PUBLIC ADMINISTRATION

The most comprehensive treatment of public administration is Andrew Dunsire, *Administration: The Word and the Science* (1973, reprinted 1981). Included among the classics in the field are Frederick Winslow Taylor, *The Principles of Scientific Management* (1911), available in numerous later editions; Henri Fayol, *General and Industrial Management*, rev. ed. (1984; originally published in French, 1917); and Max Weber, *Economy and Society: An Outline of Interpretive Sociology*, edited by Guenther Roth and Claus Wittich, 2 vol. (1978; originally published in German, 4th rev. ed., 1956). Marshall W. Meyer, *Change in Public Bureaucracies* (1979), is an important quantitative study of the process of change; and E.N. Gladden, *A History of Public Administration*, 2 vol.

(1972), is an informative survey of developments from the 11th century to the present day. For further study, useful information can be found in Jay M. Shafritz, *The Facts on File Dictionary of Public Administration* (1985); and also in Robert D. Miewald, *The Bureaucratic State: An Annotated Bibliography* (1984).

The traditional approach to public administration and its principles are set forth in Luther H. Gulick and L. Urwick (eds.), *Papers on the Science of Administration* (1937, reprinted 1987); and L. Urwick, *The Elements of Administration*, 2nd ed. (1947). Challenges to the principles, as well as efforts to build a theory of decision making as central to administration, appear in Chester I. Barnard, *The Functions of the Executive* (1938, reprinted 1979); Herbert A. Simon, *Administrative Behaviour: A Study of Decision-Making Processes in Administrative Organization*, 2nd ed. (1957, reissued 1965); and Herbert A. Simon, Donald W. Smithburg, and Victor A. Thompson, *Public Administration* (1950, reprinted 1971). A thoughtful review of the evolution of public administration in its relation to society is provided in Dwight Waldo, *The Administrative State: A Study of the Political Theory of American Public Administration*, 2nd ed. (1984). A challenge to the traditional dichotomy between policy and administration is expressed cogently in various works of Paul H. Appleby, most notably in his *Policy and Administration* (1949, reprinted 1975). Later developments of similar views are found in David B. Truman, *The Governmental Process: Political Interests and Public Opinion*, 2nd ed. (1971); Emmette S. Redford, *Democracy in the Administrative State* (1969); and Harold Seidman and Robert Gilmour, *Politics, Position and Power: From the Positive to the Regulatory State*, 4th ed. (1986). The nature and role of cost–benefit analysis is discussed in Peter Self, *Econocrats and the Policy Process: The Politics and Philosophy of Cost-Benefit Analysis* (1975). The incremental approach to decision making is set out in Charles E. Lindblom, *The Intelligence of Democracy: Decision Making Through Mutual Adjustment* (1965); the problems involved in applying techniques such as PPBS and Programme Analysis and Review are discussed in Aaron Wildavsky, *The Politics of the Budgetary Process*, 4th ed. (1984); and

Andrew Gray and William I. Jenkins, *Administrative Politics in British Government* (1985). The prophet of the human relations movement was Mary Parker Follett, some of whose writings are published in *Dynamic Administration: The Collected Papers of Mary Parker Follett*, new ed., edited by Elliot M. Fox and L. Urwick (1973, reissued 1982). The derivative movement, now called organization development, is treated in Chris Argyris, *Integrating the Individual and the Organization* (1964); Rensis Likert, *New Patterns of Management* (1961, reprinted 1987); and Warren G. Bennis, *Organization Development: Its Nature, Origins, and Prospects* (1969). A wide-ranging discussion of issues in policy analysis is provided in Brian W. Hogwood and Lewis A. Gunn, *Policy Analysis for the Real World* (1984). A growing literature has developed since World War II in case studies of actual administrative experience. Pioneered and led by the American Inter-University Case Program, the use of cases has spread to many other countries. An example of the use of cases in comparative analysis is Frederick C. Mosher (ed.), *Governmental Reorganizations: Cases and Commentary* (1967). John E. Rouse, Jr., *Public Administration in American Society: A Guide to Information Sources* (1980), is a comprehensive annotated bibliography.

On the administrative systems of different countries, see Brian Chapman, *The Profession of Government: The Public Service in Europe* (1959, reprinted 1980); F.F. Ridley (ed.), *Specialists and Generalists: A Comparative Study of the Professional Civil Servant at Home and Abroad* (1968); Fred W. Riggs, *Administration in Developing Countries: The Theory of Prismatic Society* (1964); Morroe Berger, *Bureaucracy and Society in Modern Egypt: A Study of the Higher Civil Service* (1957, reissued 1969); and Joseph La Palombara (ed.), *Bureaucracy and Political Development*, 2nd ed. (1967).

PUBLIC OPINION

Classic treatments of public opinion include William Alexander MacKinnon, *On the Rise, Progress and Present State of Public Opinion in Great Britain, and Other Parts of the World* (1828, reprinted 1971); James Bryce, *The American Commonwealth*, 2 vol. (1888, reissued 1995); Albert V. Dicey, *Lectures on the Relation Between Law & Public Opinion in England During the Nineteenth Century*, 2nd ed. (1914, reissued 1985); Charles Horton Cooley, *Social Process* (1918, reissued 1966); Walter Lippmann, *Public Opinion* (1922, reissued 2004); William Albig, *Modern Public Opinion* (1939, reissued 1956); and Leonard W. Doob, *Public Opinion and Propaganda*, 2nd ed. (1966).

The history of public opinion is traced in Harold D. Lasswell, Daniel Lerner, and Hans Speier (eds.), *Propaganda and Communication in World History*, 3 vol. (1979); John G. Geer, *From Tea Leaves to Opinion Polls: A Theory of Democratic Leadership* (1996); John R. Zaller, *The Nature and Origins of Mass Opinion* (1992); and Slavko Splichal, *Public Opinion: Developments and Controversies in the Twentieth Century* (1999).

Excellent summaries of polling theory and application are found in Sherry Devereaux Ferguson, *Researching the Public Opinion Environment: Theories and Methods* (2000); Frank Louis Rusciano et al., *World Opinion and the Emerging International Order* (1998); Paul J. Lavrakas and Michael W. Traugott, *Election Polls, the News Media, and Democracy* (2000); and Richard Hodder-Williams, *Public Opinion Polls and British Politics* (1970).

Defenses of the polling process by eminent practitioners, albeit with suggestions about how the polls might be improved, are George Gallup and Saul Forbes Rae, *The Pulse of Democracy* (1940, reissued 1968); George Gallup, *A Guide to Public Opinion Polls*, 2nd ed. (1948); Frank Teer and James D. Spence, *Political Opinion Polls* (1973); John Clemens, *Polls, Politics, and Populism* (1983); Robert M. Worcester (ed.), *Political Opinion Polling: An International Review*, 2nd ed. (2002); Leo Bogart, *Polls and the Awareness of Public Opinion*, 2nd ed. (1988); Robert M. Worcester, *British Public Opinion* (1991); Albert H. Cantril, *The Opinion Connection* (1991); and Daniel Yankelovich, *Coming to Public Judgment* (1991).

Academic critiques of polling include Lindsay Rogers, *The Pollsters: Public Opinion, Politics, and Democratic Leadership* (1949); Michael Wheeler, *Lies, Damn Lies, and Statistics: The Manipulation of Public Opinion in America* (1976); Benjamin Ginsberg, *The Captive Public: How Mass Opinion Promotes State Power* (1986); Irving Crespi, *The Public Opinion Process: How the People Speak* (1997); John Lukacs, *Democracy and Populism: Fear and Hatred* (2005); and Hanno Hardt and Slavko Splichal, trans. and eds., *Ferdinand Tönnies on Public Opinion: Selections and Analyses* (2000).

Innovative and significant works using poll data include V.O. Key, *Public Opinion and American Democracy* (1961); Ronald Inglehart, *The Silent Revolution: Changing Values and Political Styles Among Western Publics* (1977); Paul M. Sniderman, Richard A. Brody, and Phillip E. Tetlock, *Reasoning and Choice: Explorations in Political Psychology* (1991); and Elisabeth Noelle-Neumann, *The Spiral of Silence: Public Opinion, Our Social Skin*, 2nd ed. (1993; originally published in German, 1980), which tries to show how perceptions of public opinion themselves shape what individuals say and do. Policy making at the legislative and executive levels is discussed in Lawrence R. Jacobs, *The Health of Nations: Public Opinion and the Making of American and British Health Policy* (1993); Lawrence R. Jacobs and Robert Y. Shapiro, *Politicians Don't Pander: Political Manipulation and the Loss of Democratic Responsiveness* (2000); and Geoff Mulgan, *Connexity: Responsibility, Freedom, Business, and Power in the New Century* (1997).

The continuing problem of "rationality" is the focus of V.O. Key, *The Responsible Electorate: Rationality in Presidential Voting, 1936–1960* (1966); Graeme C. Moodie and Gerald Studdert-Kennedy, *Opinions, Publics, and Pressure Groups: An Essay on 'Vox Populi' and Representative Government* (1970); Benjamin I. Page, *Choices and Echoes in Presidential Elections: Rational Man and Electoral Democracy* (1978); and Benjamin I. Page and Robert Y. Shapiro, *The Rational Public: Fifty Years of Trends in Americans' Policy Preferences* (1992).

Classic studies of American elections, which reveal a great deal about public opinion, include Bernard Berelson, Paul F. Lazarsfeld, and William N. McPhee, *Voting: A Study of Opinion Formation in a Presidential Campaign* (1954, reprinted 1986); Angus Campbell, Gerald Gurin, and Warren E. Miller, *The Voter Decides* (1954, reprinted 1971); Angus Campbell et al., *The American Voter* (1960, reprinted 1980); Paul F. Lazarsfeld, Bernard Berelson, and Hazel Gaudet, *The People's Choice*, 3rd ed. (1968); and *Martin P. Wattenberg, The Rise of Candidate-Centered Politics: Presidential Elections of the 1980s* (1991). Diffusion of information and opinion leadership is discussed in Elihu Katz and Paul F. Lazarsfeld, *Personal Influence,* 2nd ed. (2006); and Todd Gitlin, "Media Sociology: The Dominant Paradigm," *Theory and Society*, 6(2):205–253 (September 1978).

INDEX

A

accountability, constitutional government and, 106–107
Adorno, Theodor, 18
Africa, constitutional government and, 118, 120
agricultural society, government and, 75–77
Almond, Gabriel, 23
American Revolution, 85
American Voter, The, 19
Aristotle, 1, 2, 3, 105, 125–126, 127
Asia, constitutional government and, 120–121

B

Bagehot, Walter, 13, 112
balloting, 70
Banfield, Edward, 23
behavioralism, 11, 13, 18–22, 23, 25, 38–39, 144, 145, 147
Bentley, Arthur F., 9, 144–145
Bertalanffy, Ludwig von, 25
Bodin, Jean, 5
Bowling Alone, 24
Bryce, James, 13
Burke, Edmund, 5, 137–138
Butler, David, 19

C

Chicago school, 9–11
China, public administration and, 101
Civic Culture, The, 23, 24
communism, 26, 29, 31, 38, 44, 87–88, 89, 100, 101, 111, 117, 140–141, 143
Comte, Auguste, 6, 10, 139–140
Confucius, 1, 25, 93, 122–124
constitutional change, constitutional government and, 110–111
constitutional government
features of, 105–113
practice of, 113–121
constitutionality, constitutional government and, 109–110
constitutional stability, constitutional government and, 112–113
constructivism, 42–43
Crozier, Michel, 18

D

Dahl, Robert A., 29, 149–151
democratic theory, 28–30
dependency theory, 16
Deutsch, Karl, 25
division of power, constitutional government and, 18

Djilas, Milovan, 12
Downs, Anthony, 27
Duverger, Maurice, 18

E

Easton, David, 25
elections
    districting and apportionment,
        65–67
    participation in, 71–73
    types of, 62–64
    vote counting, 64–65
    voting practices, 68–71, 74
Engels, Friedrich, 8, 11, 141,
    143–144
England
    constitutional government,
        113–115
    decolonization and national
        constitutions, 118
    public administration and empire,
        97–99
environment, public opinion and,
    51
Eurobarometer, 20, 22
Europe, constitutional government
    and, 116–117, 119
executive elections, vote counting
    and, 65

F

fascism, 18, 87–88
feudalism, 80–81
foreign policy analysis, overview of,
    40–41
France, public administration and,
    96–97
French Revolution, 5, 85–86, 96

G

general-system perspective, 41–42
Gore, Al, 55, 68
government, 21st-century, 89–90
Greek city-states, 2, 78, 126

H

Hitler, Adolf, 12, 88, 106, 108, 111,
    117, 119
Hobbes, Thomas, 4, 130, 135
Huntington, Samuel, 27, 29

I

Ibn Khaldun, 1, 127–128
imperialism, rise of, 86

interest groups, public opinion and, 53

international political economy, overview of, 43–45

international relations
early history of, 31–33
and integration, 38–39
modern, 39–45
post-World War I, 33–34
post-World War II, 34–38

Latin America, constitutional government and, 120

legislative elections, vote counting and, 64

Lenin, Vladimir Ilich, 87–88

liberal democracy, 88–89

Lijphart, Arend, 29

Linz, Juan, 29

Lipset, Seymour, 24, 29

Locke, John, 4, 132–133

J

Japan, public administration and, 101–102

K

Kaplan, Morton, 26

Kautilya, 1, 126–127

Key, V.O., Jr., 19, 46, 59, 147

Kjellén, Rudolf, 12

L

Lasswell, Harold Dwight, 10, 18, 25, 145–147

M

Machiavelli, Niccolò, 3–4, 127, 129

Marx, Karl, 8, 11, 12, 16, 31, 43, 44, 45, 88, 140–41, 143, 144

mass media, public opinion and, 51–53

Merriam, Charles, 10

Michels, Robert, 12

Middle Ages, government and, 79–81

monarchy
absolute, 83–84
constitutional, 84

Montesquieu, 5, 135–136

Moral Basis of a Backward Society, The, 23

Morgenthau, Hans, 11, 37, 38

Mosca, Gaetano, 12

N

nationalism, rise of, 86
nation-state, origins of, 81
neoliberalism, 42
neorealism, 42
North Atlantic Treaty Organization
(NATO), 35, 36

O

O'Donnell, Guillermo, 20
opinion leaders, public opinion and,
53–54
Ostrogorsky, Moisey, 13

P

Pareto, Vilfredo, 12
Parsons, Talcott, 25
Plato, 1–2, 23, 124–125, 127
Political Change in Britain, 20
political culture, overview of, 23–25
political polls, 53, 58, 60–61
political science, history of,
ancient, 1–3
early modern, 3–5
19th-century, 6–8
20th-century, 8–12, 15

Political System, The, 25
procedural stability, constitutional
government and, 106
Prussia, public administration and,
95–96
public administration
and developing nations, 102–104
early systems, 91–92, 94–95
public opinion
formation of, 49–50
and government, 56–60
influences, 51–56
polling, 53, 58, 60–61
theories of, 46–49
Putnam, Robert, 24

R

rational choice theory, 27–28
realism, postwar, 37–38
representation, constitutional
government and, 107
Ricardo, David, 44, 45
Riker, William, 27–28, 148–149
Rokkan, Stein, 20
Roman Republic, 78–79
Rousseau, Jean-Jacques, 4–5, 107,
133–134
Russia, public administration and,
100

S

Saint-Simon, Henri de, 6, 138–139
Siegfried, André, 13
Smith, Adam, 5, 44, 45, 136–137
Song dynasty, 92–93, 94
Stalin, Joseph, 11, 88, 106, 117
Stokes, Donald, 19
structure-institution debate, 42
Survey Research Center, 19
systems analysis, 12, 25–27

T

Tingsten, Herbert, 13
Tocqueville, Alexis de, 6–8, 12, 23, 24
transparency, constitutional government and, 108

U

United States
constitutional government and, 116
public administration and, 99–100

V

Valenzuela, Arturo, 16, 20
Verba, Sidney, 23
voter identification laws, 72
voting
compulsory, 70–71
corrupt practices, 71
influences on voting behaviour, 74
secret, 69–70

W

Weber, Max, 12, 15, 18
Wilson, Woodrow, 9, 31, 54